Go Global

English for Global Business

Garry Pearson   Graham Skerritt   Hiroshi YOSHIZUKA

photographs by
© iStockphoto

音声ファイルのダウンロード

CDマーク表示がある箇所は、音声を弊社HPより無料でダウンロードすることができます。トップページのバナーをクリックし、書籍検索してください。書籍詳細ページに音声ダウンロードアイコンがございますのでそちらから自習用音声としてご活用ください。

https://www.seibido.co.jp

Go Global

Copyright © 2019 Global Bridge (KK Pearson Enterprises)
http://www.globalbridge.co.jp

All rights reserved for Japan.
No part of this book may be reproduced in any form
without permission from Seibido Co., Ltd.

Preface

Most leading Japanese companies are trying to expand their business overseas. In order to do so, their employees need to be able to communicate with their business partners, including coworkers, customers and suppliers, in these countries. This generally means that employees need to be able to use English for work. However, just being able to communicate in English is not enough. To be successful in business, it is very important to be able to communicate in an appropriate way – using formal, semi-formal, or casual language in both speaking and writing.

After training thousands of business professionals with Global Bridge (one of Japan's leading corporate training companies), we know the language that employees need to work in a global company. We wrote "Go Global" to teach you how to communicate professionally and build better relationships with your business partners all over the world.

Good luck in your future career.

Garry Pearson
Graham Skerritt
Hiroshi YOSHIZUKA

The Structure of a Business Email

A good business email typically has seven parts. Using this structure will ensure your email is professional and easy to understand. In this course, you will learn how to write the different parts of a good business email.

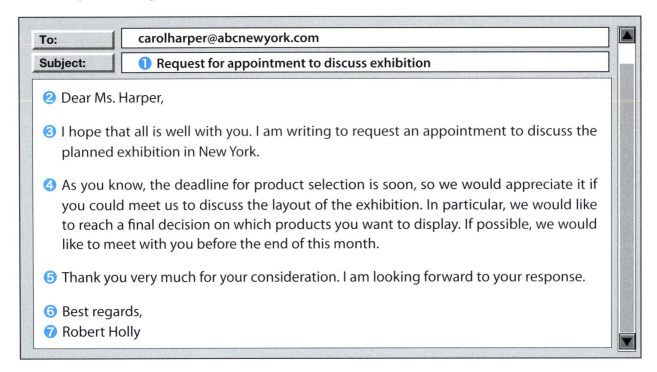

❶ Subject Line
The subject line should give the reader a clear idea of the contents of the email before they actually open the mail, but it needs to be short. (See page 42 for more information.)

❷ Salutation
The salutation is a greeting that needs to be appropriate for the level of formality of the email. (See pages 11 and 53 for more information.)

❸ Opening Paragraph
The opening paragraph includes a friendly comment and the explains purpose of the email. (See pages 17 and 84 for more information.)

❹ Body
The body is the main content of the email. It can be divided into paragraphs, but should not include too much information. (See pages 29 and 36 for more information.)

❺ Closing Paragraph
The closing paragraph contains another friendly comment and may suggest next actions. (See pages 48 and 78 for more information.)

❻ Valediction
The valediction is the words we use to end the email, and they should be appropriate to the level of formality. (See page 23 for more information.)

❼ Your Name
There are different ways to write your name depending on the level of formality. (See page 5 for more information.)

Level of Formality: Choosing between Formal, Semi-Formal and Casual

When communicating in business, it is important to consider the level of formality. Using very casual language with a senior member of staff can make you sound unprofessional, whereas using very formal language with a coworker can make you sound unfriendly. So how can you choose the correct level of formality?

Business writing can be divided into three types:

- **FORMAL WRITING**: This is very polite and respectful, but can seem unfriendly if we are communicating with people we are close with.
- **CASUAL WRITING**: This is very natural and friendly and sometimes resembles spoken English, but can seem disrespectful if we are communicating with very senior or important people.
- **SEMI-FORMAL WRITING**: This is a balance between the two and is most commonly used in business situations. It is polite and respectful, but at the same time friendly.

To choose the correct level of formality, think about these two questions:

1. *What is your relationship with the other person?*
How well do you know them? If you know each other well, you have a "close relationship." If you have never met or you barely know each other, you have a "distant relationship."

2. *What is the position of the other person?*
Is the person junior or senior to you, or at the same level as you?

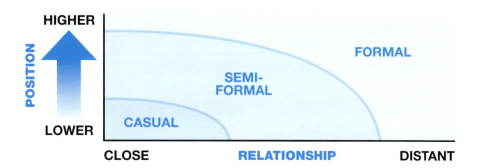

If you are ever unsure which level to use, it is safer to use a semi-formal tone, because this is appropriate for most business situations. However, think carefully about the content of your message. For example, if you are discussing a very serious topic or making a difficult request, you may want to use a more formal tone.

In this course, you will learn formal, semi-formal and casual expressions for many types of email. However, remember to choose an appropriate level of formality <u>before</u> writing your email.

EnglishCentralのご案内

本テキスト各ユニットの「Conversation」と「Supplementary Worksheet」で学習した会話音声は、オンライン学習システム「EnglishCentral」で学習することができます。EnglishCentralでは動画の視聴や単語のディクテーションのほか、動画のセリフを音読し録音すると、コンピュータが発音を判定します。PCだけでなく、スマートフォンのアプリからも学習できます。リスニング、スピーキング、語彙力向上のため、ぜひ活用してください。EnglishCentralの利用にはアカウントとアクセスコードの登録が必要です。登録方法については下記ページにアクセスしてください。

（画像はすべてサンプルで、実際の教材とは異なります）

https://www.seibido.co.jp/np/englishcentral/blended.html

見る
- 本文内でわからなかった単語は1クリックでその場で意味を確認
- スロー再生
- 日英字幕（ON/OFF可）

学ぶ
- 音声を聴いて空欄の単語をタイピング。ゲーム感覚で楽しく単語を覚える

話す
- 動画のセリフを音読し録音、コンピュータが発音を判定。
- 日本人向けに専門開発された音声認識によってスピーキング力を％で判定
- ネイティブと自分が録音した発音を聞き比べ練習に生かすことができます
- 苦手な発音記号を的確に判断し、単語を緑、黄、赤の3色で表示

CONTENTS

Unit 1	Introducing Yourself	1
Unit 2	Introducing Companies	7
Unit 3	Explaining Your Role	13
Unit 4	Introducing Products	19
Unit 5	Checking Information	25
Unit 6	Giving Your Opinion	31
Unit 7	Making Requests	37
Unit 8	Asking Permission	43
Unit 9	Making Invitations	49
Unit 10	Making Appointments	55
Unit 11	Canceling and Rescheduling	61
Unit 12	Describing Locations	67
Unit 13	Looking after a Visitor	73
Unit 14	Making a Phone Call	79
Unit 15	Taking Messages	85
Supplementary Worksheets		91
Useful Vocabulary List		106

UNIT 1 Introducing Yourself

GOAL ✓

Learn how to introduce yourself to coworkers and business contacts

1 Vocabulary

Match the underlined words to the meanings.

1. I majored in English literature at university. (   )
2. I started a new job and my new coworkers bought me lunch. (   )
3. She recently started working in the IT Department. (   )
4. I have been assigned to the Sales Team. (   )
5. "Nice to meet you." "Same here." (   )

    A. the people you work with   **B.** part of a company   **C.** studied
    D. give someone a job or position   **E.** I feel the same way

2 Listening

 02

Listen to the conversation and choose the correct answer to each question.

1. Who is Tom?
   A. Miyuki's manager   **B.** Miyuki's coworker   **C.** Miyuki's friend   **D.** Miyuki's professor

2. Which area does Tom work in?
   A. Recruitment   **B.** Manufacturing   **C.** Finance   **D.** Computing

3. When did Miyuki graduate?
   A. Three years ago   **B.** Two years ago   **C.** Last year   **D.** This year

4. What was Miyuki's major?
   A. Marketing   **B.** Media   **C.** Accounting   **D.** Business Administration

1

UNIT 1 Introducing Yourself

3 | Conversation

Practice the conversation with your partner.

Tom: Hello. Are you new?

Miyuki: Yes, my name is Miyuki Hara.

Tom: It's nice to meet you. I'm Thomas Davies, but please call me Tom.

Miyuki: Nice to meet you, too, Tom. Which department do you work in?

Tom: I belong to the Accounting Division. How about you?

Miyuki: I work in the Marketing Department. I have been assigned to the Social Media Team.

Tom: Sounds interesting. So did you graduate this spring?

Miyuki: Yes, I graduated from Florida State University.

Tom: What did you study?

Miyuki: I majored in Business Administration.

Tom: Great. Well, I'd better get back to work. My coworkers are waiting for me. It was nice talking with you.

Miyuki: Same here.

4 | Useful Expressions

Complete the expressions with words from the conversation.

Telling people your name	Greeting someone for the first time
• **My name is** Miyuki Hara. • **I'm** Thomas Davies. • **Please (1)** _____ **me** Tom.	• **F**: It's a pleasure to meet you. • **S**: It's **(2)** _____ to meet you. • **C**: Good to meet you.
Telling people about your job	Telling people about your university
• **I (3)** _____ **to** the Accounting Division. • **I work in** the Marketing Department. • **I have been (4)** _____ **to** the Social Media Team.	• **I (5)** _____ **from** Florida State University. • **I studied** Business Administration. • **I majored in** Economics.

F=formal   **S**=semi-formal   **C**=casual

5 | Speaking

Make conversations for the people in the chart below. Use the conversation above to help you.

	Conversation 1	Conversation 2	Conversation 3
A	• Elizabeth Brown (Liz) • HR Department	• Jonathan Thompson (John) • Sales Division	• Katherine Black (Kate) • R&D Department
B	• Hiroshi Tanaka • IT Department • Database Team	• Mikiko Hashimoto • Legal Department • Contracts Team	• Nozomi Kagawa • Sales Department • Online Sales Team

6 Reading

Read the article and choose the correct answers to the questions.

My first week at Google

So I am officially a "Noogler," a new hire at Google!

On Monday, I arrived at the campus and went to the orientation to create my login details and have my photo taken for my employee ID. There was a long line of people waiting, but it was fine because there were some musicians playing for us! I introduced myself to some other new recruits. Some had just graduated from college like me, but others were moving to Google from other jobs.

We had two days of orientation on Tuesday and Wednesday, where we learned all about working for Google – and we also got to eat at some of the great restaurants on campus. After orientation, I was assigned a mentor – a senior coworker from my department. She took me to my desk and introduced me to the rest of our team. They were all really friendly. I'm really looking forward to working with them.

1. What is the article mainly about?
   - **A.** Looking for a new job
   - **B.** Applying for a new job
   - **C.** Starting a new job
   - **D.** Helping a new recruit

2. What did the writer NOT do on her first day?
   - **A.** Talk with other new employees
   - **B.** Set up her username and password
   - **C.** Get a picture taken
   - **D.** Meet her team members

3. What did the writer do before working at Google?
   - **A.** She worked for another company.
   - **B.** She was a university student.
   - **C.** She was a musician.
   - **D.** She worked in a restaurant.

4. In the article, the word "hire" in paragraph 1, line 1 is closest in meaning to
   - **A.** manager
   - **B.** recruit
   - **C.** mentor
   - **D.** training

3

UNIT 1 — Introducing Yourself

7 | Example Business Email

Read the **SEMI-FORMAL** email that Miyuki sent to introduce herself to her new coworkers. Check (✓) the topics she includes.

☐ age   ☐ department   ☐ hobbies   ☐ hometown   ☐ team   ☐ university course

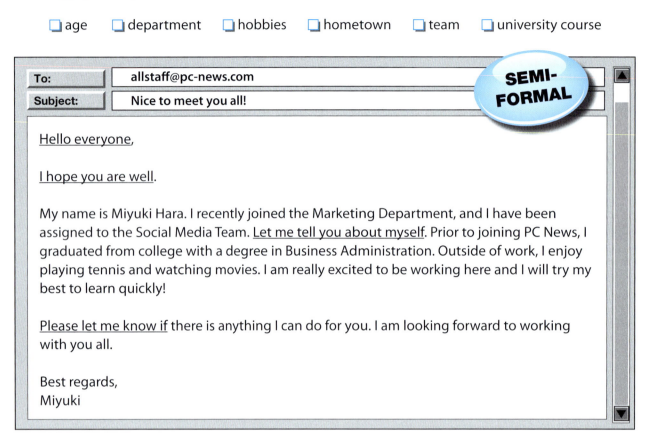

To: allstaff@pc-news.com
Subject: Nice to meet you all!

Hello everyone,

I hope you are well.

My name is Miyuki Hara. I recently joined the Marketing Department, and I have been assigned to the Social Media Team. Let me tell you about myself. Prior to joining PC News, I graduated from college with a degree in Business Administration. Outside of work, I enjoy playing tennis and watching movies. I am really excited to be working here and I will try my best to learn quickly!

Please let me know if there is anything I can do for you. I am looking forward to working with you all.

Best regards,
Miyuki

8 | Essential Email Expressions

Write **F** (formal), **S** (semi-formal), or **C** (casual) next to each expression in the chart.

Greeting people	Opening pleasantry
1. ( ) **Hello** everyone,	4. ( ) How's it going?
2. ( ) **Dear** all,	5. ( ) I hope you are well.
3. ( ) **Hi** guys,	6. ( ) I hope this email finds you well.
Introducing yourself	**Offering help**
7. ( ) Let me tell you about myself.	10. ( ) Please do not hesitate to contact me if…
8. ( ) Please allow me to introduce myself.	11. ( ) Please let me know if…
9. ( ) Here's a little about me.	12. ( ) Please feel free to ask if…

4

9 Writing Task 1

Choose the correct words and expressions to complete this **FORMAL** email from Miyuki to James Edwards, manager of the Sales Department.

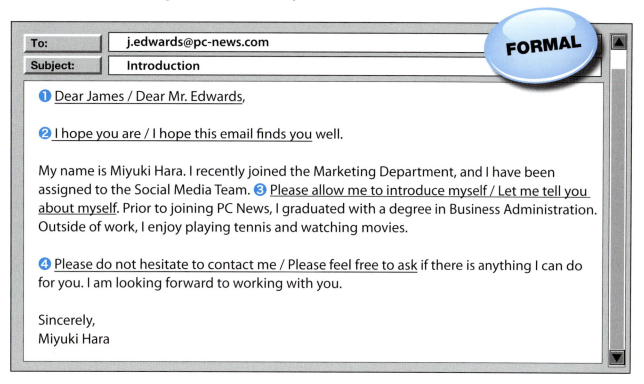

To: j.edwards@pc-news.com
Subject: Introduction

❶ Dear James / Dear Mr. Edwards,

❷ I hope you are / I hope this email finds you well.

My name is Miyuki Hara. I recently joined the Marketing Department, and I have been assigned to the Social Media Team. ❸ Please allow me to introduce myself / Let me tell you about myself. Prior to joining PC News, I graduated with a degree in Business Administration. Outside of work, I enjoy playing tennis and watching movies.

❹ Please do not hesitate to contact me / Please feel free to ask if there is anything I can do for you. I am looking forward to working with you.

Sincerely,
Miyuki Hara

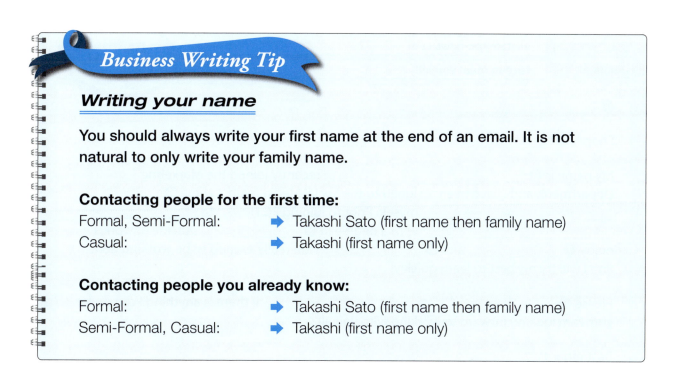

Business Writing Tip

Writing your name

You should always write your first name at the end of an email. It is not natural to only write your family name.

Contacting people for the first time:
Formal, Semi-Formal: ➡ Takashi Sato (first name then family name)
Casual: ➡ Takashi (first name only)

Contacting people you already know:
Formal: ➡ Takashi Sato (first name then family name)
Semi-Formal, Casual: ➡ Takashi (first name only)

UNIT 1 Introducing Yourself

10 | Writing Task 2

Choose the correct words and expressions to complete this **CASUAL** email from Miyuki to some coworkers that joined the company at the same time as she did.

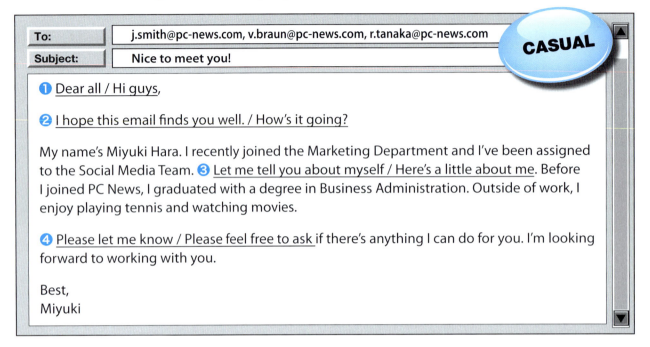

11 | Writing Task 3

Imagine that you just joined the Marketing Department at PC News. Write a **SEMI-FORMAL** email to introduce yourself to your new coworkers.

To: allstaff@pc-news.com
Subject: Nice to meet you all!

❶ _____ _____,

I hope ❷ _____ _____ _____.

My name is ❸ _____ _____. I recently joined the Marketing Department, and I have been assigned to the Social Media Team. Let me ❹ _____ _____ _____ myself. Prior to joining PC News, I ❺ _____ _____ _____ with a degree in ❻ _____. Outside of work, I enjoy ❼ _____ and ❽ _____. I am really excited to be working here and I will try my best to learn quickly!

Please ❾ _____ _____ _____ if there is anything I can do for you. I am looking forward to working with you all.

Best regards,
❿ _____ _____

UNIT 2 Introducing Companies

GOAL ✓

Learn how to explain your company to others

1 Vocabulary

Match the underlined words to the meanings.

1. We manufacture windows for cars and trains. (   )
2. They distribute books to customers all over the world. (   )
3. I have a meeting with the CEO at the company headquarters. (   )
4. Our company has branches in London and Paris. (   )
5. That bank was established in 1800. (   )

    A. shops or offices that are part of a large company   **B.** make (in a factory)
    C. started   **D.** transport   **E.** a company's main offices

2 Listening

 04

Listen to the conversation and choose the correct information to complete the business card.

Yoshi Nakamura
Sales Representative

Turner and Smith
(1) Gyms and Health Clubs / Health Food Supplier
(2) New York / Tokyo Branch

- Established in New York in (3) 1986 / 2010
- One of the leading suppliers (4) in Asia / worldwide

7

UNIT 2 — Introducing Companies

3 Conversation

  04

Practice the conversation with your partner.

Magnus: So, which company do you work for, Yoshi?

Yoshi: I work for Turner and Smith. <u>We're</u> a health food company. <u>We manufacture and distribute</u> dried fruits, nuts, and cereals. Let me give you my card.

Magnus: Is that an American company?

Yoshi: Yes, <u>our headquarters is located in</u> New York, but <u>we have</u> fifteen <u>branches</u> worldwide. I work for the Japan branch in Tokyo.

Magnus: Sounds interesting. Is it a new company?

Yoshi: Actually, <u>it was established in</u> New York in 1986, but <u>the Japan branch opened in</u> 2010.

Magnus: And how's business?

Yoshi: Very good. <u>We're one of the leading</u> health food suppliers in Asia.

4 Useful Expressions

Complete the expressions with words from the conversation.

Explaining the main business	Giving details about the company
• **We're a** health food **(1)** _____ . • **We provide** financial services. • **We manufacture** electronic appliances.	• **Our headquarters is (2)** _____ **in** New York. • **We have branches in** 15 countries. • **We employ about** 2,000 **people** worldwide.
Explaining the company history	**Explaining success**
• **We were (3)** _____ **in** 1986. • **We were founded by** Takeshi Mori. • **The Japan branch opened in** 2010.	• **We are one of the (4)** _____ banks in Japan. • **We are the market leader in** Asia. • **We received an award for** our customer service.

5 Speaking

Make similar conversations to the one above using these business cards.

Sora Kitano
Junior Reporter

Daily Financial News
Berlin Branch

- 24-hour financial news channel
- Established New York, 1975
- Branches: London (from 1980), Paris (from 1985), Berlin (from 1990), Tokyo (from 2000)

Toru Fukushima
Research Assistant

Super Cars
Osaka Branch

- Manufacturer of luxury cars
- Established Tokyo, 1990
- Branches: Osaka (from 2000), Nagoya (from 2001)

6 Reading

Read the article and choose the correct answers to the questions.

The Oldest Companies in the World

A survey by the Bank of Korea found that more than 5,000 companies around the world were more than 200 years old – and more than 3,000 of these companies were in the same country: Japan. However, the oldest company in the world was founded a lot more than 200 years ago.

Kongō Gumi Ltd. is a construction company that builds Buddhist temples – although they also helped to construct Osaka Castle. Amazingly, the company was established in Osaka in the year 578. They operated as an independent company for over 1,400 years before being taken over by a larger company in 2006.

The second oldest company in the world is also in Japan. Nishiyama Onsen Keiunkan is a hot spring hotel in Yamanashi Prefecture with 37 rooms. It was founded in 705 and has been looking after guests for more than 1,300 years. It is a family-run hotel that has been run by 52 generations of the same family.

The third oldest company is another hotel in Japan. The Koman Hotel in Hyōgo Prefecture was founded in 717 in Kinosaki – an area famous for its hot springs and bathhouses.

1. What kind of company is the oldest company in the world?
   A. It's a bank.
   B. It's a construction company.
   C. It's a hotel.
   D. It's a bathhouse.

2. According to the article, about how many companies in Japan are more than 200 years old?
   A. 5,000
   B. 3,000
   C. 1,400
   D. 200

3. What is NOT true about Kongō Gumi Ltd.?
   A. It was established in Osaka.
   B. It is now owned by another company.
   C. It mainly builds castles.
   D. It was established over 1,400 years ago.

4. What is indicated about the two hotels?
   A. They have the same number of rooms.
   B. They were founded in the same year.
   C. They are both in areas with hot springs.
   D. They are both in the same prefecture.

UNIT 2 Introducing Companies

7 | Example Business Email

Read this **FORMAL** email. Who did Yoshi send this to? Why did Yoshi send it?

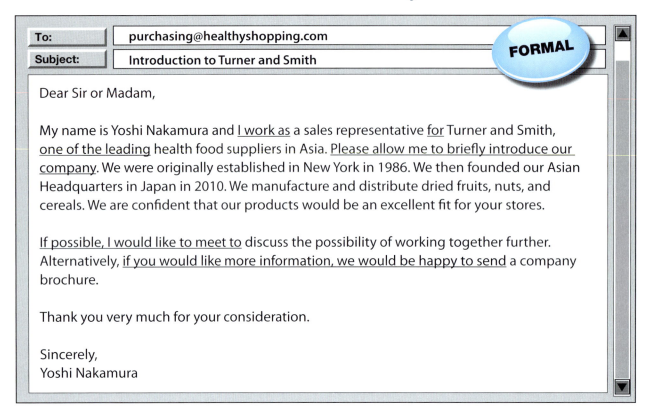

To: purchasing@healthyshopping.com
Subject: Introduction to Turner and Smith

FORMAL

Dear Sir or Madam,

My name is Yoshi Nakamura and <u>I work as</u> a sales representative <u>for</u> Turner and Smith, <u>one of the leading</u> health food suppliers in Asia. <u>Please allow me to briefly introduce our company</u>. We were originally established in New York in 1986. We then founded our Asian Headquarters in Japan in 2010. We manufacture and distribute dried fruits, nuts, and cereals. We are confident that our products would be an excellent fit for your stores.

<u>If possible, I would like to meet to</u> discuss the possibility of working together further. Alternatively, <u>if you would like more information, we would be happy to send</u> a company brochure.

Thank you very much for your consideration.

Sincerely,
Yoshi Nakamura

8 | Essential Email Expressions

Write **F** (formal), **S** (semi-formal), or **C** (casual) next to each expression in the chart.

Introducing your position	Introducing your company
1. ( ) **I'm a** sales rep **at** Turner and Smith.	4. ( ) Let me (quickly) tell you about…
2. ( ) **I am** a marketer **for** Apple.	5. ( ) I would like to (briefly) introduce…
3. ( ) **I work as an** engineer **for** Toyota.	6. ( ) Please allow me to introduce…
Asking for an appointment	**Offering information**
7. ( ) Can we meet to… ?	10. ( ) We can send…
8. ( ) If possible, I would like to meet to…	11. ( ) If you would like more information, we would be happy to send…
9. ( ) Could we meet to… ?	12. ( ) If you are interested, we could send…

9 Writing Task 1

Choose the correct expressions to complete this **SEMI-FORMAL** email from Yoshi to a health food company.

Business Writing Tip

Salutations

At the start of an email, you need to greet the person you are writing to and write their name.

- For a **casual** email, use *Hi* + their first name: *Hi Anna,*
- For a **semi-formal** email, use *Dear* + their first name: *Dear Anna,*
- For a **formal** email, use *Dear* + *Mr.* or *Ms.* + their second name: *Dear Mr. Jones,*
- If you don't know the person's name, use *Dear* + *Sir* or *Madam*: *Dear Sir* or *Madam,*

UNIT 2 — Introducing Companies

10 | Writing Task 2

Imagine you are writing to a potential customer. Complete this **FORMAL** email with the information from the chart.

Your company name:	Apple Inc.
Company information:	Established in 1976; 123,000 employees
Company description:	Technology company, producer of consumer electronics
Your job:	Sales representative

To: John.Smith@potential.com
Subject: Introduction to Apple Inc.

FORMAL

Dear ❶ _____ _____,

I hope this email ❷ _____ _____ well.

My name is ❸ _____ _____, and I work as a ❹ _____ _____ for ❺ _____ Inc., one of the leading ❻ _____ _____ in the world. Please allow me to briefly introduce our company. We were originally established in ❼ _____ and currently employ ❽ _____ people. We are one of the leading producers of electronic consumer goods in the world. We are confident that our products would be an excellent fit for your stores.

If possible, ❾ _____ _____ _____ _____ meet to discuss our products. Alternatively, if you would like more information, we would be happy to send a company brochure.

Thank you very much for your consideration.

Sincerely,
❿ _____ _____

UNIT 3
Explaining Your Role

GOAL ✓

Learn how to explain your job and the work of your team

1 Vocabulary

Match the underlined words to the meanings.

1. We sent a questionnaire to customers to get their feedback. (   )
2. Companies need to do regular maintenance of essential equipment. (   )
3. The quality control process found a problem with this machine. (   )
4. Please ensure the products are sent to the customer today. (   )
5. I am in charge of electrical products. (   )

   A. checking that products are good enough to sell
   B. a set of questions that you ask people for research
   C. make sure
   D. making sure that machines are in good condition and fixing them
   E. in control of

2 Listening

 06

Listen to the conversation and decide if the sentences are true (T) or false (F).

1. Motohiro and Karen are friends. (   )
2. Motohiro works in a junior role in the company. (   )
3. His team mainly conducts market research in Japan. (   )
4. At the moment, he is analyzing feedback about some clothing. (   )
5. Karen's department contains three different teams. (   )
6. Karen is the manager of her department. (   )

UNIT 3 | Explaining Your Role

3 | Conversation

  06

Practice the conversation with your partner.

Karen: Hi. Nice to meet you. I'm Karen.

Motohiro: Nice to meet you, too. I'm Motohiro. I just started working here last week.

Karen: Well, welcome to the company. So what do you do here?

Motohiro: I'm a research assistant in the Market Research Department. My team is responsible for research in Europe. I send out questionnaires to key customers and then analyze the data. We're currently looking at customer feedback on our new range of sportswear.

Karen: That sounds very interesting.

Motohiro: And can I ask which department you work for?

Karen: I work for the manufacturing department. We're divided into three teams: the production team, the maintenance team, and the quality control team. I manage the quality control team, so I'm in charge of ensuring that our products are good enough to be sold.

Motohiro: I see.

4 | Useful Expressions

Look at the expressions below and find three sentences a salesperson could say, three sentences a receptionist could say, and three sentences a marketing executive could say.

Describing your responsibilities	Describing your main tasks
• **I'm responsible for** sales in Europe. • **I'm in charge of** greeting visitors. • **We oversee** the creation of commercials.	• **I analyze** market research data. • **I organize meetings** for senior coworkers. • **I ensure** all visitors sign in and out.
Explaining your current projects	**Explaining the structure of your team**
• **I am currently working on** a deal with a supplier in South America. • **We're developing** some new software. • **We're preparing to** launch a new website.	• **The** Sales **Department is divided into** three teams of four people. • **We're divided into** three **teams:** online marketing, catalogues, and magazine ads. • **There are** six receptionists **on the team**.

5 | Speaking

Create a similar conversation to the one above for these people:

1. a salesperson and a marketing executive
2. a receptionist and a research assistant

14

6 Reading

Read the article and choose the correct answers to the questions.

Crazy Job Titles: Good or Bad?

Have you ever been given a business card by someone whose job is "rockstar" or "ninja"? These days, many businesses, especially those in the technology sector, are finding that it can be motivating for staff to have fun job titles. Younger people don't want boring job titles, such as "receptionist" or "system engineer." They want playful titles that make them sound interesting, important, and creative. Who wants to be a receptionist when you can be a "Director of First Impressions"? Who wants to be system engineer when you can be a "Technology Ninja"?

However, although it sounds like a fun idea, it's actually not good for your business because it makes it hard to know what anyone in the company actually does. For example, job ads that use these crazy job titles sound fun, but applicants might not understand what the job involves and this could prevent good people from applying. Another problem is that customers have no idea who to contact when they need help with something. Finally, there can also be confusion within the company. Without clear roles, people might not agree on who is responsible for what. Think about a rock concert. If you want the concert to be successful, you need technicians, ticket sellers, managers, and security staff. Not everyone can be rockstars.

1. Which kinds of companies often use crazy job titles?
   - **A.** Music companies
   - **B.** Technology companies
   - **C.** Engineering companies
   - **D.** Recruitment companies

2. What do younger people think about job titles like "rockstar" and "ninja"?
   - **A.** They think they are crazy.
   - **B.** They think they are boring.
   - **C.** They think they are fun.
   - **D.** They think they are confusing.

3. What is suggested about using crazy job titles?
   - **A.** All businesses should use them.
   - **B.** They are only suitable for creative jobs.
   - **C.** Customers like them.
   - **D.** Companies should not use them.

4. What disadvantage of using crazy job titles is NOT mentioned?
   - **A.** Staff are not serious about work.
   - **B.** It's harder to recruit the right people.
   - **C.** Customers do not know who to talk to.
   - **D.** Staff do not understand their roles.

UNIT 3   Explaining Your Role

7 | Example Business Email

Read this **SEMI-FORMAL** email from Motohiro to a coworker. Which region does Motohiro organize research for?

| To: | kwilliams@premiumsportsgoods.com |
| Subject: | Introduction of Market Research Department |

Dear Keith,

Thank you for your enquiry about the Market Research Department. My name is Motohiro Hasebe and I have been asked to support you.

The department is divided into three teams, with each team responsible for one region. Our team oversees Europe, while the two other teams manage North America and Asia Pacific. Our role is to collect information from our customers, analyze the data, and provide insights to our Product Development and Sales Divisions.

If there is ever anything we can do for you, please feel free to contact us. We would be happy to help you with any questions.

Best regards,
Motohiro

8 | Essential Email Expressions

Write **F** (formal), **S** (semi-formal), or **C** (casual) next to each expression in the chart.

Thanking for contact	Explaining department structure
1. ( ) **Thank you for** your call today.	4. ( ) **We have** three **teams in our department**.
2. ( ) **Thank you very much for** your email.	5. ( ) **The department consists of** three **teams**.
3. ( ) **Thanks for** your message.	6. ( ) **There are** three **teams in our department**.
Explaining the role of your team	**Offering help**
7. ( ) **Our role is to** collect data.	10. ( ) We would be happy to help.
8. ( ) **Our main job is** to collect data.	11. ( ) It would be our pleasure to help you.
9. ( ) **Our primary function is to** collect data.	12. ( ) We'd be happy to help.

16

9 Writing Task 1

Choose the correct words and expressions to complete this **FORMAL** email from Motohiro to the new manager of the Corporate Communications Division.

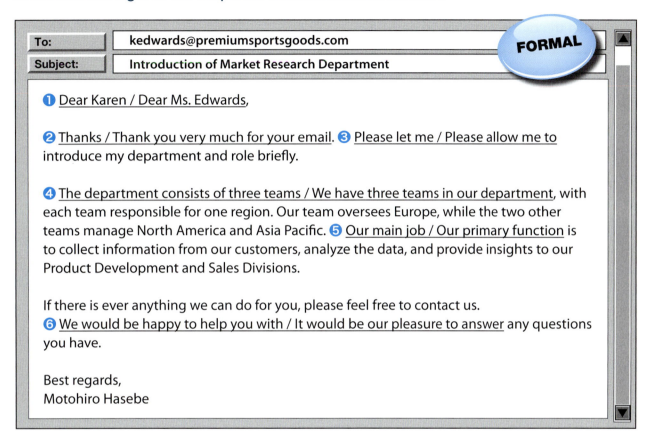

Business Writing Tip

Opening Pleasantries

It's polite to start an email with a friendly greeting. Here are three good ways to write greetings:

If you don't know the person well, use a general greeting:
- I hope you are well.
- I hope this email finds you well.

If you know the person well, use a more personalized greeting:
- I hope you had a good holiday.
- I hope the weather in New York is nice.

If you are replying to an email, use:
- Thank you for your email.
- Thank you for your message.

UNIT 3 — Explaining Your Role

10 | Writing Task 2

Imagine that you are Tomoko Shibata and you work in the Online Marketing Team for a soft drink company. A new employee, Jack Saunders, has asked for information about your department. Complete this **SEMI-FORMAL** email to introduce your department and your team. Use the diagram below to help you.

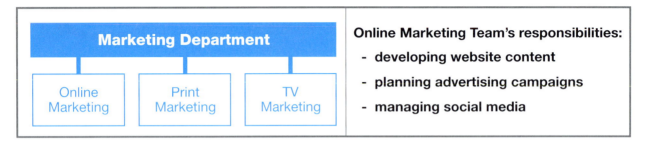

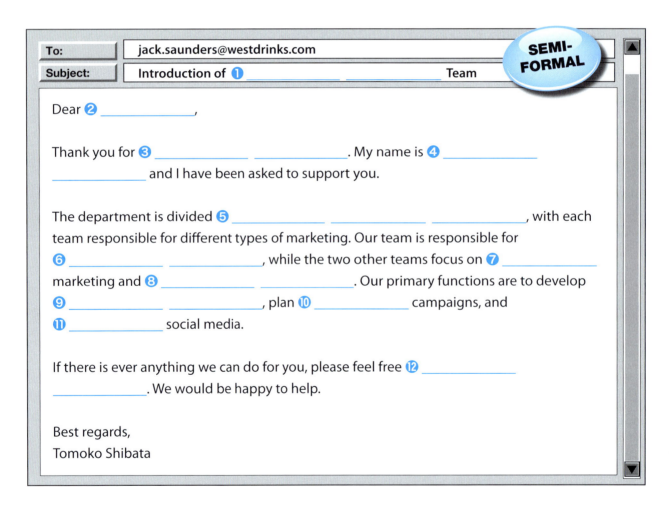

To: jack.saunders@westdrinks.com
Subject: Introduction of ❶ _____ _____ Team

SEMI-FORMAL

Dear ❷ _____,

Thank you for ❸ _____ _____. My name is ❹ _____ _____ and I have been asked to support you.

The department is divided ❺ _____ _____ _____, with each team responsible for different types of marketing. Our team is responsible for ❻ _____ _____, while the two other teams focus on ❼ _____ marketing and ❽ _____ _____. Our primary functions are to develop ❾ _____ _____, plan ❿ _____ campaigns, and ⓫ _____ social media.

If there is ever anything we can do for you, please feel free ⓬ _____ _____. We would be happy to help.

Best regards,
Tomoko Shibata

UNIT 4 Introducing Products

GOAL ✓

Learn how to explain the benefits and features of your products

1 Vocabulary

Match the underlined words to the meanings.

1. Toyota is famous for producing state-of-the-art cars. (   )
2. This shop sells home appliances like blenders and washing machines. (   )
3. Can you tell me the dimensions of this TV? (   )
4. We have upgraded our TVs so they are even better than before. (   )
5. It comes with instructions. (   )

    A. using modern technology or knowledge   **B.** information about how to do something
    C. the length, width, or height of something   **D.** electronic devices you use in the house
    E. improved

2 Listening

 08

Listen to Hideki explaining his company's products and complete the information.

Bread Making Machines	
Basic Model	**Deluxe Model**
• 30 cm high x ❶ _____ cm wide x ❷ _____ cm long • Made of ❸ _____ plastic • LCD display and ❹ _____ • Book of ❺ _____ recipes	• ❻ _____ cm high x 30 cm wide x 30 cm long • Made of ❼ _____ • LCD display and ❽ _____ • Book of ❾ _____ recipes

19

UNIT 4 — Introducing Products

3 | Conversation

Practice the conversation with your partner.

Sylvie: So, what do you do, Hideki?

Hideki: I'm a sales rep for a home appliance manufacturer in Japan.

Sylvie: What kind of products do you make?

Hideki: Well, we mainly produce kitchen appliances, such as blenders and bread making machines.

Sylvie: Really? What kinds of bread making machines do you have?

Hideki: We sell two different models. The basic model is made of white plastic and it's 30 cm high by 25 cm wide by 25 cm long. It comes with a book of 10 recipes. It also has an LCD display and a timer, so you can use it to cook bread for you while you sleep.

Sylvie: That sounds really useful.

Hideki: We also have a deluxe model. It's state-of-the-art. It's made of stainless steel and its dimensions are 35 cm high by 30 cm wide by 30 cm long. Like the basic model, it has an LCD display and a timer. However, it comes with a book of 25 recipes and you can use it to make cakes as well as bread. It's one of our most popular products.

Sylvie: It sounds a little complicated. I hope it comes with instructions!

4 | Useful Expressions

Complete the expressions with words from the conversation

Describing the product	Explaining key features
• It's (1) _____ _____ white plastic. • **Its dimensions are** / **It's** 30 **cm high by** 30 **cm wide by** 30 **cm long**. • **It's very** stylish / compact / traditional.	• It (2) _____ _____ a book of 10 recipes. • It (3) _____ an LCD display and a timer. • **It features** an LCD display.
Explaining the use	**Giving facts about the products**
• **It makes** 10 different recipes. • **You can** (4) _____ _____ to make cakes. • **It lets you** cook bread while you sleep.	• **It's one of** our (5) _____ popular _____. • **It's one of** the best-selling brands in Japan. • **It's** our latest model.

5 | Speaking

Choose a real company. Describe some of this company's products to your partner – but do not say the name of the company. Can your partner guess which company you chose?

You can choose:
- a clothing manufacturer
- a home appliances manufacturer
- a computer company
- a software company
- a drinks company
- a snacks company

6 Reading

Read the article and choose the correct answers to the questions.

Features versus Benefits

When you describe a product to a customer, you can talk about its features (what it is and what it can do) and its benefits (how it helps the customer). Although it is useful to describe the features, it is essential to explain the benefits. This is particularly important in marketing messages. Bad marketing focuses on the features. Good marketing highlights the benefits.

This problem happens because companies often think that everyone will automatically be interested in their great new product. However, there are a lot of other companies telling them about other great products, too. If you want customers to buy your product, you need to show them how it can help them or solve their problems. They need to know the benefits.

For example, when Apple launched the iPod in 2001, one of its key features was the industry-first 5GB hard drive. However, their marketing slogan focused on the benefit to the customer: "1,000 songs in your pocket." This was a much more effective way to help the customer understand why they should buy this product.

1. What does a benefit describe?
   - **A.** The product
   - **B.** The product's key features
   - **C.** How the product is useful
   - **D.** The customer

2. What problem do bad marketing messages have?
   - **A.** They do not describe the features.
   - **B.** They do not describe the benefits.
   - **C.** They do not show pictures of the product.
   - **D.** They do not appeal to everyone.

3. According to the article, how should companies get people to notice a product?
   - **A.** Show them the product
   - **B.** Compare it to other products
   - **C.** Highlight the new features
   - **D.** Show how it will help them

4. What customer problem did Apple's iPod slogan highlight?
   - **A.** They wanted to carry more music.
   - **B.** They wanted a cheaper price.
   - **C.** They wanted to understand the technology.
   - **D.** They wanted to find new music.

UNIT 4 | Introducing Products

7 | Example Business Email

Read this **SEMI-FORMAL** email from Hideki to a customer he knows well. Choose the best subject line.

To:	jrodriguez@kitchenstores.com
Subject:	Request for a meeting / Introduction of our latest model / Enquiry about new model

SEMI-FORMAL

Dear Jorge,

I hope you are well.

<u>I am writing to tell you about</u> our new deluxe bread making machine. <u>I am available to</u> come to your store to demonstrate the product for you.

Our stylish new deluxe bread making machine is state-of-the-art. It's made of stainless steel and measures 35 cm high by 30 cm wide by 30 cm long. It features an LCD display with a timer, so customers can wake up to fresh bread every morning. It also comes with a book of 25 delicious recipes, including some great cakes as well as bread.

For more information, please see the attached brochure. <u>I would be happy to</u> answer any questions you have. <u>I hope to hear from you soon.</u>

Best regards,
Hideki Fujimori

8 | Essential Email Expressions

Complete the chart with expressions from the email.

Introducing a new product	Offering a next step
F: I would like to inform you about … **S**: I am (1) _____ _____ _____ you about …. **C**: I'm writing to let you know about …	**F**: I would be very happy to … **S**: I am (2) _____ to …. **C**: I can …
Inviting questions	**Closing pleasantry**
F: Please do not hesitate to ask if you have any questions. **S**: I (3) _____ _____ to answer any questions you have. **C**: Please ask if you have any questions.	**F**: I look forward to hearing from you soon. **S**: (4) _____ _____ to hear from you soon. **C**: Hope to hear from you soon.

22

9 | Writing Task 1

Choose the correct expressions to complete this **CASUAL** email from Hideki to a coworker.

To: lisa.barnes@tokyokitchen.com
Subject: Details about new bread making machine

CASUAL

❶ <u>Dear / Hi</u> Lisa,

Hope you're well.

I am writing to ❷ <u>inform you / let you know</u> about our new deluxe bread making machine. I ❸ <u>can / would be very happy to</u> come to your next team meeting to ❹ <u>demonstrate the product for you / show you the product</u>.

The new deluxe bread making machine is made of stainless steel and measures 35 cm high by 30 cm wide by 30 cm long. It features an LCD display with a timer, so customers can wake up to fresh bread every morning. It also comes with a book of 25 delicious recipes, including some great cakes as well as bread.

For more ❺ <u>info / information</u>, please see the attached brochure. Please ❻ <u>ask / do not hesitate to ask</u> if you have any questions.

❼ <u>I look forward to hearing / Hope to hear</u> from you soon.

Best,
Hideki

Business Writing Tip

Valedictions

Every business letter or email should include a valediction, which is a short phrase at the end of an email before your name. Valediction means "saying farewell" and is used to show respect. Here are some commonly used phrases:

- **Formal**: Sincerely yours, (American English),
  Yours sincerely, (British English)

- **Semi-Formal**: Regards, Best regards, (most common)
  Kind regards, (friendlier)

- **Casual**: Thanks, Best, (Mostly American English)
  Cheers, (Mostly British English)

UNIT 4 — Introducing Products

10 | Writing Task 2

Hideki is writing a **FORMAL** email to a potential new customer. Complete the email with the information below.

New product information	
Product	Smartphone
Material	black aluminium
Size	14 cm (high) x 7 cm (wide) x 0.5 cm (thick)
Features	• updated camera • very light
Benefits	• takes amazing photos • easy to carry

To: info@megaphone.com
Subject: Introduction of our new smartphone

FORMAL

Dear Sir or Madam,

I hope this email finds you well.

I would like to inform you about our new ❶ _____. I would be ❷ _____ _____ _____ visit your store to demonstrate it for you.

Our new model is made of ❸ _____ _____ and measures ❹ _____ high by ❺ _____ wide – and it's only ❻ _____ cm thick. It includes an ❼ _____ _____, so you can ❽ _____ _____ photographs. It's also incredibly light, so it's very ❾ _____ _____ carry.

For more information, please refer to the attached brochure. Please do not ❿ _____ _____ _____ if you have any questions.

I look forward to ⓫ _____ from you soon.

Sincerely,
Hideki Fujimori

UNIT 5
Checking Information

GOAL ✓

Learn how to check information when you cannot hear or cannot understand

1 Vocabulary

Match the underlined words to the meanings.

1. I asked him to <u>elaborate</u> on his point. (   )
2. Could you <u>reword</u> this for me? I can't understand. (   )
3. I would like to <u>clarify</u> one point. (   )
4. Ms. Silver called to <u>confirm</u> the delivery date. (   )
5. Please don't <u>interrupt</u> the presentation. Ask questions at the end. (   )

    A. express something using different words

    B. say something while another person is talking

    C. say if something is true or correct

    D. explain in more detail

    E. make something clear or clearer

2 Listening

 10

Yuri is talking to her manager, James. Listen to the conversation and choose the correct answers to the questions.

1. What does James ask Yuri to do?
    - **A.** Attend a conference on Friday
    - **B.** Organize a new day and time for a meeting
    - **C.** Have a meeting with some customers

2. When does James want to speak to Mr. Desmond and Ms. Shaw?
    - **A.** Any time on Friday
    - **B.** Friday morning
    - **C.** Any time this morning

UNIT 5 Checking Information

3 Conversation

  10

Practice the conversation with your partner.

James: Yuri, can you arrange a conference call with Mr. Desmond and Ms. Shaw for me? I need–

Yuri: I'm sorry to interrupt, but could you repeat that, please?

James: Can you contact Mr. Desmond and Ms. Shaw and arrange a conference call for me?

Yuri: Sorry, I'm not sure what you mean by conference call. Could you reword that?

James: It means a phone meeting.

Yuri: Ah! OK. Thank you for clarifying. I understand now.

James: OK. Please ask them to meet with me on Friday.

Yuri: Sure. What is the meeting about? Could you elaborate?

James: I want to ask them about upcoming business trips.

Yuri: OK. May I confirm that? You're saying that you want to speak to Mr. Desmond and Ms. Shaw about upcoming business trips on Friday. Is that right?

James: Yes, that's right.

4 Useful Expressions

Practice saying the expressions. Then look at the conversation again. What does Yuri say to interrupt? What does she say to show that she understands?

Saying you didn't hear	Saying you didn't understand
• Could you repeat that, please? • Could you speak a little slower, please? • Could you speak a little louder, please?	• Could you reword that? • I'm not sure what you mean. • I don't understand.
Asking questions to check	**Checking your understanding**
• What does "conference call" mean? • I don't know that word. Could you spell it? • Could you elaborate?	• In other words, you mean… Is that correct? • May I confirm? You're saying… • If my understanding is correct, you mean…

5 Speaking

Ask your partner these questions and write down their answers. If you can't hear or don't understand their answers, use the expressions above to help you.

1. Where is your hometown? What kind of place is it?
2. What is your favorite class at university? Why do you like it?
3. Do you enjoy studying English? Why?/Why not?

6 Reading

Read the article and choose the correct answers to the questions.

The Importance of Asking Questions

When a new employee joins my company, I always give them the same advice: if they do not understand something, they should always ask. Some people think they will look bad if they ask questions, but they could look much worse if they do not. Let me give you two examples.

Several years ago, when we were a much smaller company, I asked my assistant to buy some cakes for the team to celebrate the end of a project. I asked her to get 15 cupcakes while I was in a meeting and gave her the company credit card. She looked a little confused, but she didn't say anything. Anyway, when I came out of the meeting, there were cupcakes all over the office. I asked her how many she bought and she said 50. She misheard me and was too embarrassed to check. I was not happy.

Another time, a member of our sales team went to Tokyo for a month to do some research. I asked him to call me at 9 a.m. every Thursday to give me an update. However, on his first week, he called me at 1 a.m. in the morning. I was worried and asked him if everything was OK. He said, "It's 9 a.m. so I'm calling for our meeting."

1. Who is the writer of this article?
   A. A new employee at a big company
   B. A translator
   C. A government worker
   D. The CEO of a company

2. Why does the writer think that people do not ask questions?
   A. They are too busy.
   B. They think they will look foolish.
   C. They cannot speak English.
   D. They understand everything.

3. What mistake did the assistant make?
   A. She bought the wrong thing.
   B. She missed a meeting.
   C. She bought the wrong number of things.
   D. She ate the wrong cake.

4. What mistake did the salesperson make?
   A. He went to the wrong place.
   B. He phoned at the wrong time.
   C. He phoned the wrong person.
   D. His information was wrong.

UNIT 5 — Checking Information

7 | Example Business Email

Yuri received an email that she did not understand. Read her **SEMI-FORMAL** reply. What two things did she not understand?

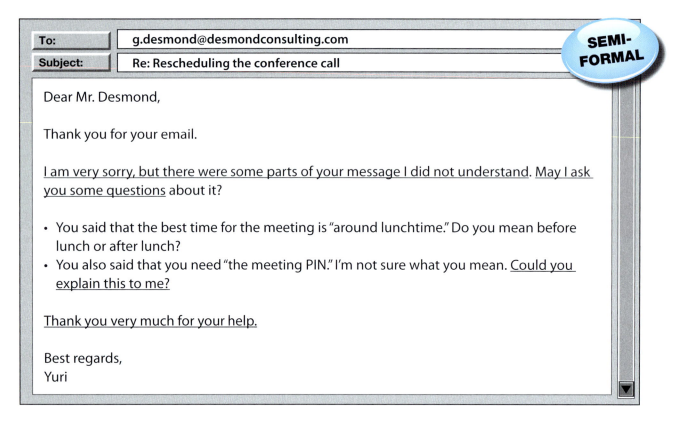

| To: | g.desmond@desmondconsulting.com |
| Subject: | Re: Rescheduling the conference call |

Dear Mr. Desmond,

Thank you for your email.

I am very sorry, but there were some parts of your message I did not understand. May I ask you some questions about it?

- You said that the best time for the meeting is "around lunchtime." Do you mean before lunch or after lunch?
- You also said that you need "the meeting PIN." I'm not sure what you mean. Could you explain this to me?

Thank you very much for your help.

Best regards,
Yuri

8 | Essential Email Expressions

Write **F** (formal), **S** (semi-formal), or **C** (casual) next to each expression in the chart.

Explaining you don't understand	Asking for help
1. ( ) I am afraid there were some parts of your message that I was unable to understand.	4. ( ) Can I check a few things?
2. ( ) I'm sorry, but I didn't understand a few parts of your message.	5. ( ) Would you mind if I asked you some questions?
3. ( ) I am very sorry, but there were some parts of your message I did not understand.	6. ( ) May I ask you some questions?
Asking for an explanation	**Thanking**
7. ( ) Can you tell me what this means?	10. ( ) I appreciate your assistance.
8. ( ) Could you explain this to me?	11. ( ) Thank you very much for your help.
9. ( ) Would you be able to explain this to me?	12. ( ) Thanks for your help.

9 | Writing Task 1

Choose the correct words to complete this **CASUAL** email from Yuri to her coworker.

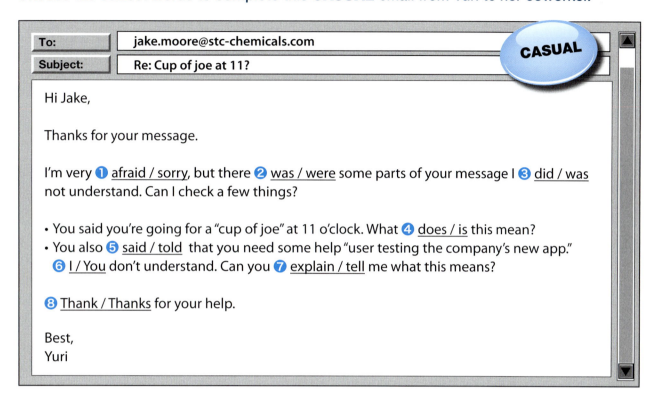

To: jake.moore@stc-chemicals.com
Subject: Re: Cup of joe at 11?

Hi Jake,

Thanks for your message.

I'm very ❶ afraid / sorry, but there ❷ was / were some parts of your message I ❸ did / was not understand. Can I check a few things?

- You said you're going for a "cup of joe" at 11 o'clock. What ❹ does / is this mean?
- You also ❺ said / told that you need some help "user testing the company's new app." ❻ I / You don't understand. Can you ❼ explain / tell me what this means?

❽ Thank / Thanks for your help.

Best,
Yuri

Business Writing Tip

Using Lists

Look at these two emails. Which is better? Why?

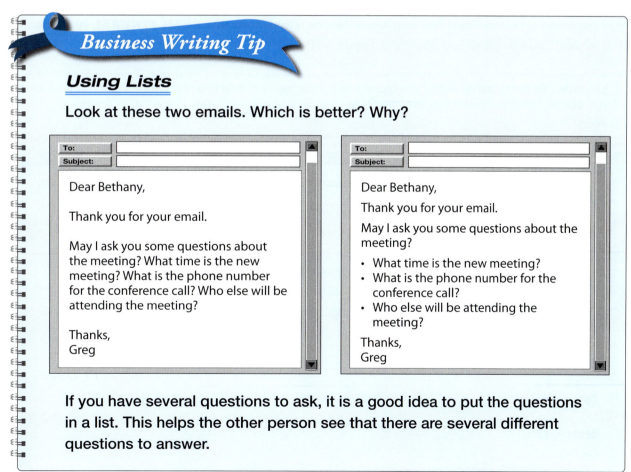

Dear Bethany,

Thank you for your email.

May I ask you some questions about the meeting? What time is the new meeting? What is the phone number for the conference call? Who else will be attending the meeting?

Thanks,
Greg

Dear Bethany,

Thank you for your email.

May I ask you some questions about the meeting?
- What time is the new meeting?
- What is the phone number for the conference call?
- Who else will be attending the meeting?

Thanks,
Greg

If you have several questions to ask, it is a good idea to put the questions in a list. This helps the other person see that there are several different questions to answer.

29

UNIT 5 | Checking Information

10 | Writing Task 2

Yuri is writing to an important customer. Correct the underlined words in her email to make it a more **FORMAL** email.

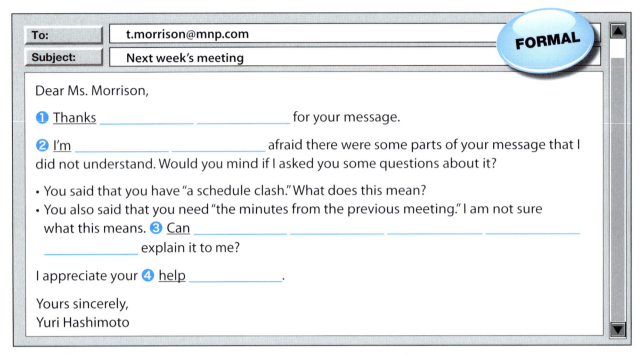

11 | Writing Task 3

Yuri received an email from her manager, James. Complete this **SEMI-FORMAL** reply asking him to clarify two things: How many paper clips should she order? Where is the customer code?

Can you order some paper clips? We usually use a company called Premier Office Equipment. You can order online, but you need the customer code.
James

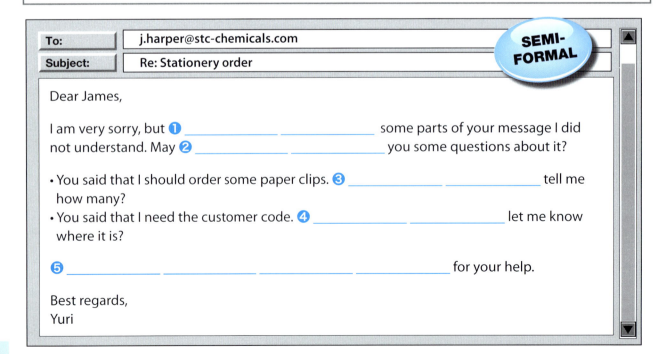

Giving Your Opinion

GOAL ✓

Learn how to give your opinion clearly

1 Vocabulary

Match the underlined words to the meanings.

1. <u>As you know</u>, I will transfer to another division next week. (   )
2. She spent her childhood in Australia. <u>Therefore</u>, she speaks English very fluently. (   )
3. <u>According to</u> the weather forecast, it will rain tomorrow. (   )
4. The food is delicious and <u>on top of that</u> it's cheap. (   )
5. You can buy good souvenirs here. <u>For instance</u>, they have some great t-shirts. (   )

    A. based on information from   **B.** for example   **C.** you remember that
    D. because of that   **E.** also

2 Listening

 12

An important customer is visiting Tokyo next week. Peter is asking Saori for ideas to entertain their visitor. Listen and make notes about her idea.

1. Where does she suggest going?

   _____

2. Why does she think they should go there?

   _____

31

UNIT 6 Giving Your Opinion

3 Conversation   12

Practice the conversation with your partner.

Peter: Saori, can I ask your opinion? As you know, Mr. Chen is visiting the office next week and he's a really important customer. Therefore, I'd like to take him somewhere special while he's here. Where do you think we should take him?

Saori: Well, <u>I think</u> we should go to Shinjuku, <u>because</u> we can take him to see the cherry blossoms in Shinjuku Park. <u>According to</u> the forecast, the weather will be really nice, so Mr. Chen can take some great pictures of the cherry blossoms. On top of that, we can eat out at a nice restaurant nearby. <u>For instance</u>, I know a great shabu shabu restaurant. <u>So</u>, I think we should go to Shinjuku.

Peter: That's a great idea. Thank you.

4 Useful Expressions

Use PREP to give clear opinions. First, say your **position** (opinion), then give the **reason** for your opinion. Then use some **expansion** (an example, some facts, or use *if* ...). Finally, say your **position** again at the end. Use the sentences in the chart to make three more suggestions for places to take Mr. Chen.

POSITION	*A weak opinion:* **Perhaps** we should go to Odaiba ... *A normal opinion:* **I think** we should go to Shibuya ... *A confident opinion:* **I strongly** believe that we should go to Ueno ...
REASON	• ... **because** we can show him the famous crossing. • ... **since** there are a lot of interesting places to visit there. • ... **as** there are a lot of interesting shops there.
EXPANSION	• *Give an example:* **For example/instance**, we could go to the National Museum. • *Refer to facts:* **According to** the news, it's a popular sightseeing spot for tourists. • *Explain the impact:* **If** we go there, he can buy some interesting souvenirs.
POSITION	• **So/Therefore**, maybe we should go to Odaiba. • **That's why** I think we should go to Shibuya. • **So, for that reason**, I believe we should go to Ueno.

5 Speaking

Prepare answers to these questions using PREP. Then ask your partner the questions.

- Where's the best city to visit in Japan?
- What's the best food for a visitor to try?
- What's the best gift to buy from Japan?
- What's the best season to visit Japan?

6 Reading

Read the article and choose the correct answers to the questions.

Let's Get Straight to the Point

Although people prefer not to state their opinions directly in some countries, in global business it is better to make sure your opinion is very clear to everyone – whether you are speaking or writing an email. This helps to prevent misunderstanding and confusion.

For example, in Japan, it is common to use the *kishoutenketsu* structure for opinions. In this structure, the speaker starts off with an introduction of the topic (*ki*), then gives information about the topic (*shou*), and offers a contrasting idea (*ten*) before coming to a conclusion (*ketsu*). This structure works well in countries where it's important not to be too direct, but it could cause misunderstanding in a global setting.

In global business, it is more common for people to state their opinion first and then explain the reasons for that opinion. This helps the speaker to get people's attention and encourages them to keep listening to understand the reasons.

When people from countries other than Japan listen to an opinion using the *kishoutenketsu* structure, they do not understand what point the speaker is trying to make and may become frustrated and confused while waiting to find out what it is. So, to avoid misunderstandings, it is safer to use PREP (Position, Reason, Expansion, Position) for global business.

1. What is the purpose of the article?
   - **A.** To tell people to not give opinions
   - **B.** To tell people to give opinions indirectly
   - **C.** To tell people to give opinions directly
   - **D.** To tell people to give opinions by email

2. In the article, the word "state" in paragraph 1, line 1 is closest in meaning to
   - **A.** ask
   - **B.** say
   - **C.** feel
   - **D.** listen

3. What is NOT true about the *kishoutenketsu* structure?
   - **A.** The conclusion comes at the end.
   - **B.** It is popular in Japan.
   - **C.** It includes a contrasting idea.
   - **D.** The opinion is stated first.

4. Why should people use the PREP structure in global business?
   - **A.** To make sure people understand
   - **B.** To stop people finding out your opinion
   - **C.** To make sure people listen carefully
   - **D.** To avoid giving your opinion

UNIT 6 | Giving Your Opinion

7 | Example Business Email

Saori's manager asked her to suggest a restaurant to go to with a visitor from England. Read the **SEMI-FORMAL** email to her manager below. What is her idea? What are the reasons for her idea?

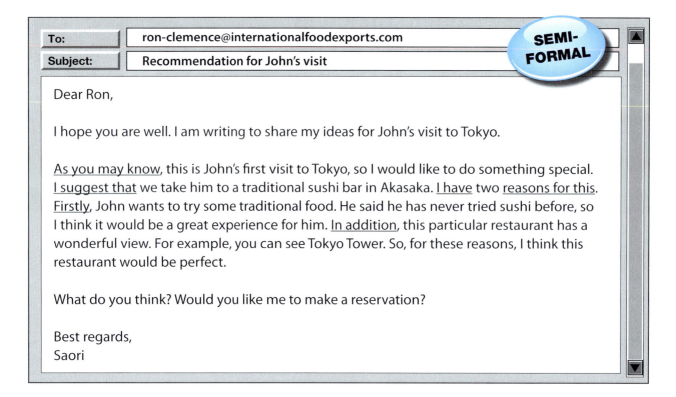

To: ron-clemence@internationalfoodexports.com
Subject: Recommendation for John's visit

Dear Ron,

I hope you are well. I am writing to share my ideas for John's visit to Tokyo.

As you may know, this is John's first visit to Tokyo, so I would like to do something special. I suggest that we take him to a traditional sushi bar in Akasaka. I have two reasons for this. Firstly, John wants to try some traditional food. He said he has never tried sushi before, so I think it would be a great experience for him. In addition, this particular restaurant has a wonderful view. For example, you can see Tokyo Tower. So, for these reasons, I think this restaurant would be perfect.

What do you think? Would you like me to make a reservation?

Best regards,
Saori

8 | Essential Email Expressions

Complete the chart with expressions from the email.

Recapping background information	Making suggestions
F: As you may be aware, this is… **S**: (1) _____ _____ _____ _____, this is… **C**: You know that this is…	**F**: I would suggest that we visit… **S**: (2) I _____ _____ we visit… **C**: You should…

Explaining structure	Listing points

F: I feel this way for two reasons…
 S: (3) _____ _____
  two _____ _____
  _____
 C: There are two reasons for this.
	• *First point:* To begin with / (4) _____ / First
	 • *Other points:* (5) _____ _____ / Secondly / Next
	 • *Last point:* Finally / Lastly / Last

9 | Writing Task 1

Choose the correct expressions to complete this **CASUAL** email from Saori to her friend.

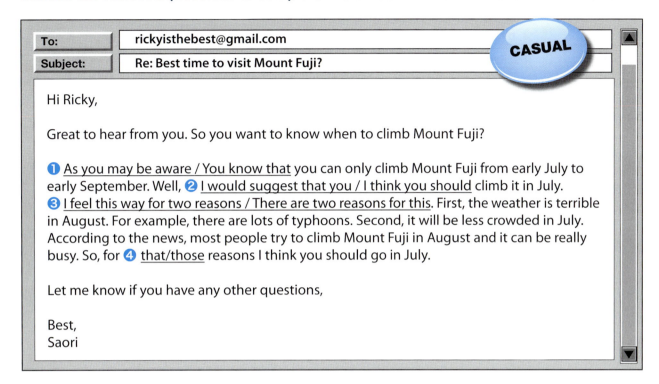

| To: | rickyisthebest@gmail.com |
| Subject: | Re: Best time to visit Mount Fuji? |

Hi Ricky,

Great to hear from you. So you want to know when to climb Mount Fuji?

❶ <u>As you may be aware / You know that</u> you can only climb Mount Fuji from early July to early September. Well, ❷ <u>I would suggest that you / I think you should</u> climb it in July. ❸ <u>I feel this way for two reasons / There are two reasons for this</u>. First, the weather is terrible in August. For example, there are lots of typhoons. Second, it will be less crowded in July. According to the news, most people try to climb Mount Fuji in August and it can be really busy. So, for ❹ <u>that/those</u> reasons I think you should go in July.

Let me know if you have any other questions,

Best,
Saori

10 | Writing Task 2

Put the sentences in the correct order to make a **SEMI-FORMAL** email from Saori to her coworker.

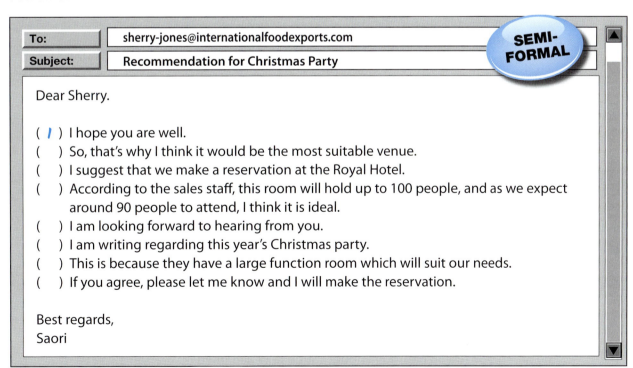

| To: | sherry-jones@internationalfoodexports.com |
| Subject: | Recommendation for Christmas Party |

Dear Sherry,

(*1*) I hope you are well.
(   ) So, that's why I think it would be the most suitable venue.
(   ) I suggest that we make a reservation at the Royal Hotel.
(   ) According to the sales staff, this room will hold up to 100 people, and as we expect around 90 people to attend, I think it is ideal.
(   ) I am looking forward to hearing from you.
(   ) I am writing regarding this year's Christmas party.
(   ) This is because they have a large function room which will suit our needs.
(   ) If you agree, please let me know and I will make the reservation.

Best regards,
Saori

35

UNIT 6 | Giving Your Opinion

11 | Writing Task 3

Complete the **FORMAL** email from Saori to a customer who is visiting Japan.

To: s_mcdonald@greengardensupplies.com
Subject: Re: Recommendation for visit to Japan

FORMAL

Dear Ms. McDonald,

Thank you for your email. I would be happy to give you some suggestions for your trip.

As you ❶ _____ _____ _____, the weather in summer is very hot, so ❷ _____ _____ _____ that you take a trip out of Tokyo to Nikko. I feel this way ❸ _____ _____ reasons. ❹ _____, it's not far. If you take the train from Shinjuku, it only takes a couple of hours. ❺ _____, you can see some beautiful scenery there. For example, there is a beautiful waterfall called Kegon Falls. ❻ _____, you can visit Toshogu Shrine. According to some guide books, it's the most beautiful shrine in Japan. So, ❼ _____ _____ _____, I think you should visit Nikko.

If you have any more questions, please do not hesitate ❽ _____ _____.

Yours sincerely,
Saori

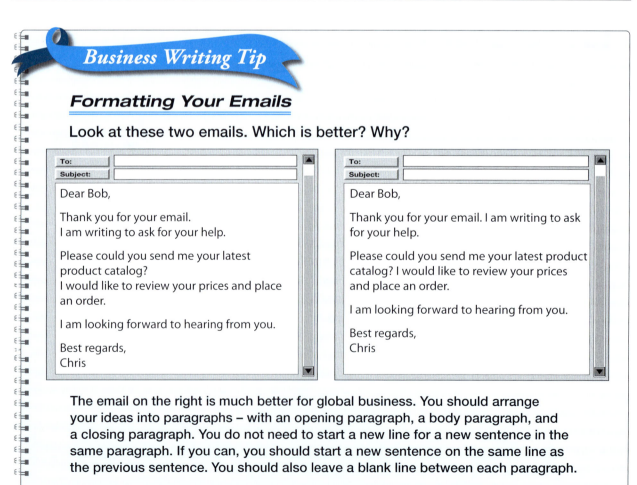

Business Writing Tip

Formatting Your Emails

Look at these two emails. Which is better? Why?

To:
Subject:

Dear Bob,

Thank you for your email.
I am writing to ask for your help.

Please could you send me your latest product catalog?
I would like to review your prices and place an order.

I am looking forward to hearing from you.

Best regards,
Chris

To:
Subject:

Dear Bob,

Thank you for your email. I am writing to ask for your help.

Please could you send me your latest product catalog? I would like to review your prices and place an order.

I am looking forward to hearing from you.

Best regards,
Chris

The email on the right is much better for global business. You should arrange your ideas into paragraphs – with an opening paragraph, a body paragraph, and a closing paragraph. You do not need to start a new line for a new sentence in the same paragraph. If you can, you should start a new sentence on the same line as the previous sentence. You should also leave a blank line between each paragraph.

UNIT 7 Making Requests

GOAL ✓

Learn how to make and respond to requests

1 Vocabulary

Match the underlined words to the meanings.

1. <u>Unfortunately</u>, I can't help you because I have a meeting now. (   )
2. <u>It's my pleasure</u>. I would be happy to help. (   )
3. Could you <u>do me a favor</u>? Can you pick up our lunch order? It's in reception now. (   )
4. <u>Absolutely</u>! When do you need me to finish? (   )
5. Thank you for your help. I really <u>appreciate</u> it. (   )

    A. do something helpful for me   **B.** feel grateful for something   **C.** Yes, of course.
    D. I'm sorry.   **E.** You're welcome.

2 Listening

 14

Naomi's manager is asking her for some help. Listen and choose the correct words to complete Naomi's to do list.

To Do List

1. ☐ Ask **Mr. Young / Mr. Young's assistant** about using the boardroom **this afternoon / this morning**.
2. ☐ **Create / Ask Stuart to create** an agenda and make **five / ten** copies.
3. ☐ Get some **tea / water** for the meeting room.

37

UNIT 7 — Making Requests

3 | Conversation

  14

Practice the conversation with your partner.

Linda: Naomi, <u>could you</u> help me set up the meeting for this afternoon?
Naomi: <u>Yes, I'd be happy to.</u> What can I do for you?
Linda: <u>Could you</u> ask Mr. Young's assistant if we can use the boardroom for our meeting?
Naomi: <u>No problem.</u> What time do we need the room?
Linda: <u>Could you</u> book it from three until five?
Naomi: <u>OK.</u> Can I help you with anything else?
LInda: Yes, we need a copy of the agenda for everyone attending the meeting. <u>Could you</u> make 10 copies?
Naomi: <u>I'd like to, but unfortunately, I can't because</u> I don't have the agenda yet.
Linda: Oh yes, that's right. <u>Could you</u> ask Stuart to make one and then print ten copies?
Naomi: <u>Sure, I'll ask</u> him right away.
Linda: And <u>if possible, could you</u> get some bottles of water for the meeting room?
Naomi: <u>Absolutely.</u>
Linda: Thank you. I really appreciate it.

4 | Useful Expressions

Circle all the phrases in the conversation that Naomi uses to accept a request.

Asking someone to do something	Refusing a request
F: **If possible, could you** book a meeting room? **S**: **Could you** book a meeting room? **C**: **Can you** book a meeting room?	**F**: I'd like to, but I'm afraid I can't because… **S**: Unfortunately, I can't because… **C**: Sorry, I can't because…
Accepting a request	**Thanking**
F: Of course, it would be my pleasure. **S**: Yes, I'd be happy to. **C**: Sure, no problem.	**F**: I really appreciate it. **S**: Thank you very much. **C**: Thanks.

5 | Speaking

Choose one of the to do lists and ask your classmates to do these tasks for you.

To Do List
- ☐ Make an agenda
- ☐ Book a meeting room
- ☐ Get a projector for the meeting room
- ☐ Take notes in the meeting

To Do List
- ☐ Greet the visitors at reception
- ☐ Get some coffee for the visitors
- ☐ Tell the visitors about our new products
- ☐ Book a taxi to take the visitors to the airport

6 Reading

Read the article and choose the correct answers to the questions.

The Importance of Saying No

If you work in an office, lots of people will ask for your help. *Could you check this report for me? Could you join this meeting? Could you look after these visitors?* If you say *yes* to every request, you will never be able to finish the things you need to do.

So how do you say *no*? First of all, say *no* politely by saying: *I'm really sorry, but I can't* or *I'd like to, but I'm afraid I can't*. It's also polite to give a reason – but make sure you keep your explanation simple: *I have another appointment* or *I have to finish this report*. You don't need to give a detailed answer – it's fine to say you have a family commitment without giving further details. However, it's important to be honest.

The other person should accept your refusal by saying: *That's OK. I understand*. You can ensure that you maintain a good relationship (and that they don't ask again) by closing the conversation with *Thanks for understanding* and getting back to work.

However, you shouldn't always say *no*. If you help others when they need your help, they will help you when you need it – so when you are able to help, say *yes*!

1. Who is this article written for?
    A. Managers **B.** Assistants **C.** Visitors **D.** All employees

2. According to the article, what kind of explanation should you give for saying no?
    A. Detailed **B.** Personal
    C. Short, but true **D.** Important

3. What should you do after the other person accepts your refusal?
    A. Tell them what to do **B.** Ask them to help you
    C. Close the door **D.** Thank them

4. When should you say yes to a request?
    A. If your manager asks you to help. **B.** If you can help.
    C. If the request is easy. **D.** You should always say no.

UNIT 7 Making Requests

7 | Example Business Email

Read this **SEMI-FORMAL** email from Naomi's customer who works in the purchasing department of a large retailer. What should Naomi do now?

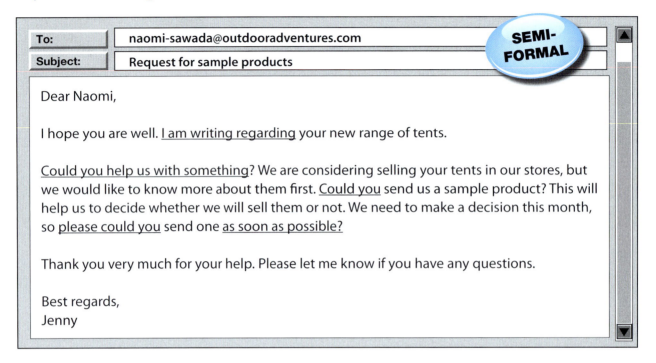

To: naomi-sawada@outdooradventures.com
Subject: Request for sample products
SEMI-FORMAL

Dear Naomi,

I hope you are well. <u>I am writing regarding</u> your new range of tents.

<u>Could you help us with something</u>? We are considering selling your tents in our stores, but we would like to know more about them first. <u>Could you</u> send us a sample product? This will help us to decide whether we will sell them or not. We need to make a decision this month, so <u>please could you</u> send one <u>as soon as possible</u>?

Thank you very much for your help. Please let me know if you have any questions.

Best regards,
Jenny

8 | Essential Email Expressions

Write **F** (formal), **S** (semi-formal), or **C** (casual) next to each expression in the chart.

Introducing the topic	Introducing a request
1. (　) **This email is in regard to** your new range of tents.	4. (　) **I was hoping you could help me** with something.
2. (　) **I'm writing about** your new range of tents.	5. (　) **Could you help me with something?**
3. (　) **I am writing regarding** your new range of tents.	6. (　) **Can you do me a favor?**

Making a request	Giving a deadline
7. (　) **Could you** send us a sample?	10. (　) **Please can you** do it **by** April 2nd?
8. (　) **Can you** send us a sample?	11. (　) **If possible, could you** finish today?
9. (　) **Would it be possible for you to** send us a sample?	12. (　) **Please could you** finish **before** 4 p.m.?

40

9 Writing Task 1

Choose the correct expressions to complete this **FORMAL** email from Naomi to a branch manager in an overseas office.

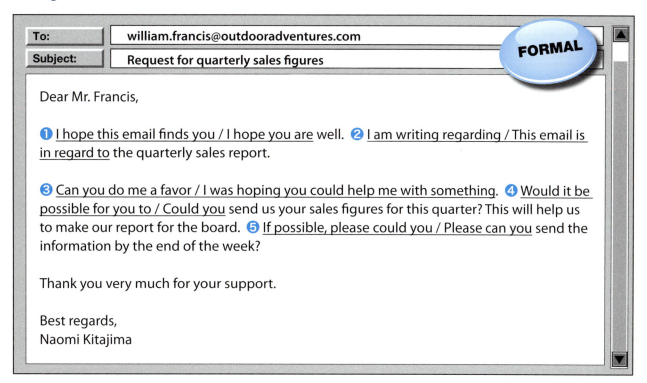

10 Writing Task 2

Choose the correct expressions to complete this **CASUAL** email from Naomi to her coworker.

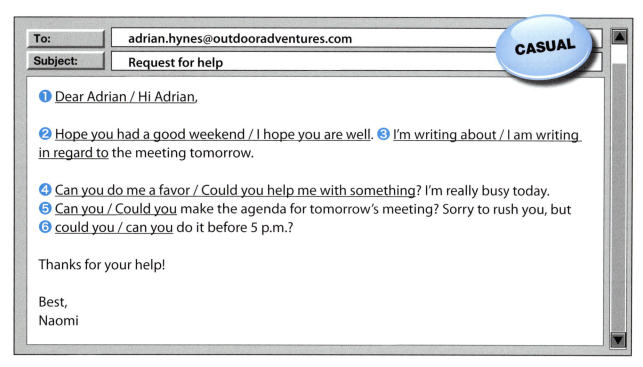

UNIT 7 — Making Requests

11 | Writing Task 3

Complete this **SEMI-FORMAL** email from Naomi to her manager.

To: andrew.griffin@outdooradventures.com
Subject: Request for budget for training

SEMI-FORMAL

❶ _____ Andrew,

I hope you are well. I am writing ❷ _____ funding for training courses.

❸ _____ _____ _____ me with something? As you know, I have been trying to improve my English and I would like to use my training budget to help me. I have found an English course in Australia that I would like to attend.

❹ _____ the company fund this course? The price is a little over ¥350,000.

❺ _____ _____ you decide before the end of July? If I can go, I need to reserve my place.

Thank you very much for your help.

Best regards,
Naomi

Business Writing Tip

Formal Subject Lines

A good way to write a clear subject for an email is to use the noun form of an action verb + a preposition + the details. You do not have to use "a" and "the" in the subject of an email.

Action Verb	Noun Form	Preposition	Details
Introduce ➡	Introduction	to	Google Inc.
Request ➡	Request	for	your latest catalog
Inquire ➡	Inquiry	about	your product prices
Apologize ➡	Apologies	for	late delivery
Thank ➡	Thanks	for	your support
Invite ➡	Invitation	to	opening ceremony
Cancel ➡	Cancelation	of	tomorrow's meeting

UNIT 8
Asking Permission

GOAL ✓

Learn how to ask for, give, and refuse permission

1 Vocabulary

Match the underlined words to the meanings.

1. Do you <u>mind</u> if I smoke here? (   )
2. "Can I use this PC?" "<u>Go ahead</u>." (   )
3. "Can I borrow your pen?" "<u>Certainly</u>." (   )
4. I'm <u>afraid</u> you can't use it now. (   )
5. "Thank you for your help." "<u>Don't mention it</u>." (   )

    A. You're welcome.   **B.** yes (casual)   **C.** yes (formal)
    D. feel unhappy   **E.** sorry

2 Listening

 16

Kaito works in the Human Resources Department of a large company. Listen and check the things on his list that he is able to do.

To Do List

1. ☐ get permission to work from home tomorrow
2. ☐ check the interview schedule
3. ☐ look at job applicants' resumes
4. ☐ book a meeting room for the interview on Friday

43

UNIT 8   Asking Permission

3 | Conversation

  16

Practice the conversations with your partner.

(1) Kaito: Excuse me, Jack.
    Jack: Yes. How can I help you?
    Kaito: <u>Would you mind, if I</u> worked from home tomorrow? I need to write some job advertisements for those new sales positions. I'll finish them quicker at home.
    Jack: <u>Yes, that's fine.</u>
    Kaito: <u>Thank you. I really appreciate it.</u>

---

(2) Kaito: Sue, <u>can I</u> look at the interview schedule for the research position?
    Sue: <u>I'm afraid you can't.</u> Greg's looking at it at the moment.
    Kaito: Oh, OK. <u>Can I</u> look at the applicants' resumes then?
    Sue: <u>Certainly.</u>
    Kaito: Thanks.

---

(3) Kaito: Sean, <u>could I</u> use Meeting Room 4 for an interview on Friday?
    Sean: <u>Sure, go ahead.</u>
    Kaito: <u>Thank you very much.</u>
    Sean: Don't mention it.

4 | Useful Expressions

In which conversation is Kaito talking to:

- a junior coworker ( )
- a coworker ( )
- his manager ( )

Asking permission	Refusing permission
F: **Would you mind if I** used this? **S**: **Could I** open the window? **C**: **Can I** borrow your pen?	**F**: I'm afraid you can't. **S**: I'm very sorry, but you can't. **C**: Sorry, you can't.
Giving permission	**Thanking**
F: Certainly. **S**: Yes, that's fine. **C**: Sure, go ahead.	**F**: Thank you. I really appreciate it. **S**: Thank you very much. **C**: Thanks.

5 | Speaking

Roll a dice three times: once to decide the person, once to decide the question, and once to decide the answer. Then make conversations like the ones above.

	⚀	⚁	⚂	⚃	⚄	⚅
1. Person	Friend	Coworker	Manager	Customer	CEO	VIP
2. Question	borrow ...	use ...	see ...	go to ...	have ...	take ...
3. Answer	Yes	Yes	Yes	No	No	No

Student A: Can I borrow your pencil?   **Student B:** Sure, go ahead.

6 Reading

Read the article and choose the correct answers to the questions.

What is GDPR?

GDPR stands for General Data Protection Regulation. In 2018, Europe introduced these new rules about data protection to ensure that companies keep personal information about their customers safe and secure. Companies can be punished if they do not manage their customer's information in the right way.

So what do companies need to do? There are three main rules.

First, all companies need to clearly state how they will use customer information when they request it. They also need to ask permission for how they will use this information. For example, they must ask customers if they want to receive information about special offers by email. Companies also need to be very careful about collecting information from children. Children under the age of 16 need to have permission from a parent or guardian.

Second, companies need to make sure they protect customer information from hackers. If customer information is stolen from a company, they may have to pay a fine. They also have to contact customers to tell them if any of their personal information was stolen.

Third, companies need to make it easy for customers to see what information the company has about them, and they also need to make it easy for customers to ask for this information to be deleted.

1. Who is this article written for?
   A. Customers
   B. IT workers
   C. Parents
   D. Companies

2. What is the purpose of the new rules?
   A. To protect companies
   B. To punish companies
   C. To protect customers
   D. To punish hackers

3. What will likely happen if customer information is stolen from a company?
   A. The company will have to close.
   B. The company will be punished.
   C. The company will delete the information.
   D. The company will not tell customers.

4. In the article, the word "guardian" in paragraph 3, line 5 is closest in meaning to
   A. teacher
   B. employee
   C. carer
   D. guard

UNIT 8　Asking Permission

7 | Example Business Email

Read this **SEMI-FORMAL** email from Kaito to his manager. What does Kaito want to do?

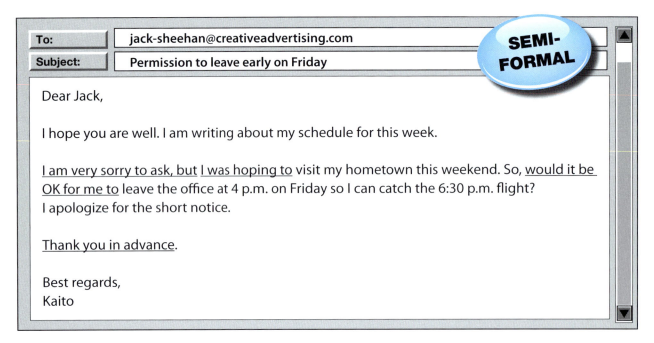

To: jack-sheehan@creativeadvertising.com
Subject: Permission to leave early on Friday

Dear Jack,

I hope you are well. I am writing about my schedule for this week.

I am very sorry to ask, but I was hoping to visit my hometown this weekend. So, would it be OK for me to leave the office at 4 p.m. on Friday so I can catch the 6:30 p.m. flight? I apologize for the short notice.

Thank you in advance.

Best regards,
Kaito

8 | Essential Email Expressions

Write **F** (formal), **S** (semi-formal), or **C** (casual) next to each expression in the chart.

Introducing a request	Explaining the reason for your request
1. (　) I am sorry to trouble you, but…	4. (　) **I would like to** visit my hometown.
2. (　) I hate to ask, but…	5. (　) **I was hoping to** visit my hometown.
3. (　) I am sorry to ask, but…	6. (　) **I have / want to** visit my hometown.
Asking permission	**Thanking (before the reader accepts)**
7. (　) If possible, would I be able to…	10. (　) Thanks in advance.
8. (　) Can I…?	11. (　) Thank you for your consideration.
9. (　) Would it be OK for me to…?	12. (　) Thank you in advance.

46

9 Writing Task 1

Choose the correct expressions to complete this **FORMAL** email from Kaito to a customer.

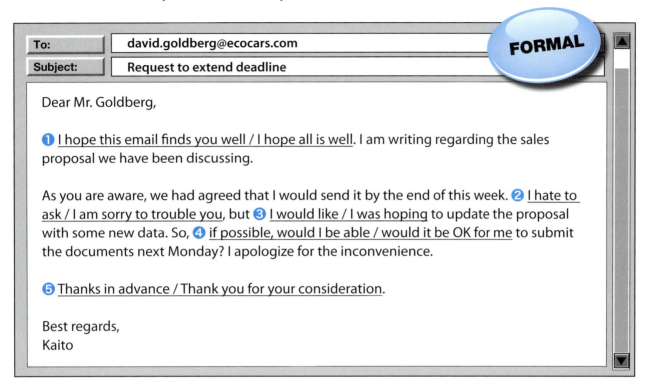

To: david.goldberg@ecocars.com
Subject: Request to extend deadline

Dear Mr. Goldberg,

❶ I hope this email finds you well / I hope all is well. I am writing regarding the sales proposal we have been discussing.

As you are aware, we had agreed that I would send it by the end of this week. ❷ I hate to ask / I am sorry to trouble you, but ❸ I would like / I was hoping to update the proposal with some new data. So, ❹ if possible, would I be able / would it be OK for me to submit the documents next Monday? I apologize for the inconvenience.

❺ Thanks in advance / Thank you for your consideration.

Best regards,
Kaito

10 Writing Task 2

Choose the correct expressions to complete this **CASUAL** email from Kaito to a coworker.

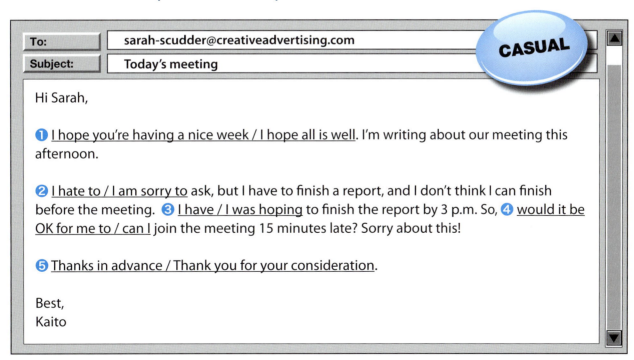

To: sarah-scudder@creativeadvertising.com
Subject: Today's meeting

Hi Sarah,

❶ I hope you're having a nice week / I hope all is well. I'm writing about our meeting this afternoon.

❷ I hate to / I am sorry to ask, but I have to finish a report, and I don't think I can finish before the meeting. ❸ I have / I was hoping to finish the report by 3 p.m. So, ❹ would it be OK for me to / can I join the meeting 15 minutes late? Sorry about this!

❺ Thanks in advance / Thank you for your consideration.

Best,
Kaito

UNIT 8 | Asking Permission

11 | Writing Task 3

Complete this **SEMI-FORMAL** email from Kaito to his manager, who is away on a business trip.

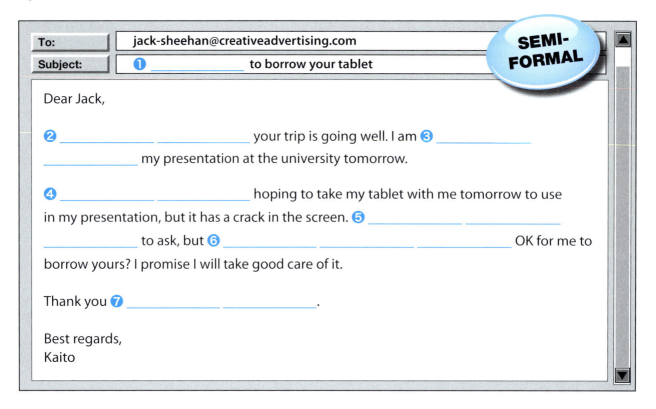

To: jack-sheehan@creativeadvertising.com
Subject: ❶ _____ to borrow your tablet

SEMI-FORMAL

Dear Jack,

❷ _____ _____ your trip is going well. I am ❸ _____ _____ my presentation at the university tomorrow.

❹ _____ _____ hoping to take my tablet with me tomorrow to use in my presentation, but it has a crack in the screen. ❺ _____ _____ _____ to ask, but ❻ _____ _____ _____ OK for me to borrow yours? I promise I will take good care of it.

Thank you ❼ _____ _____ .

Best regards,
Kaito

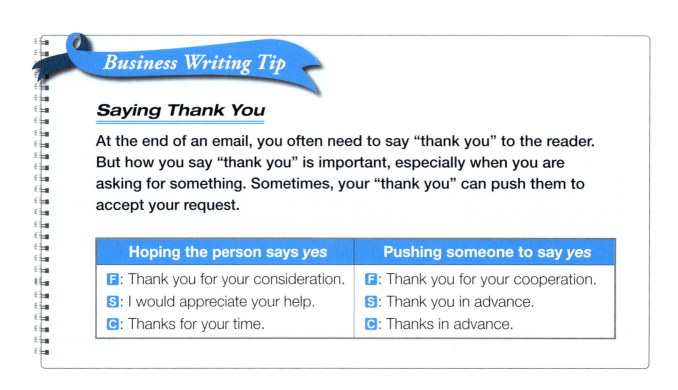

Business Writing Tip

Saying Thank You

At the end of an email, you often need to say "thank you" to the reader. But how you say "thank you" is important, especially when you are asking for something. Sometimes, your "thank you" can push them to accept your request.

Hoping the person says *yes*	Pushing someone to say *yes*
F: Thank you for your consideration.	F: Thank you for your cooperation.
S: I would appreciate your help.	S: Thank you in advance.
C: Thanks for your time.	C: Thanks in advance.

48

UNIT 9
Making Invitations

GOAL ✓

Learn how to make, refuse, and accept invitations

1 Vocabulary

Match the underlined words to the meanings.

1. I was wondering if you would like to have lunch next week. (   )
2. Where is the meeting on Friday? Do you have the details? (   )
3. "How are you?" "Couldn't be better." (   )
4. "Sorry, I can't come to the party." "That's a shame." (   )
5. "Let's go for coffee." "Sorry, I'm busy. Perhaps another time." (   )

    A. on a different day   **B.** information   **C.** unfortunate
    D. very well   **E.** interested in knowing something

2 Listening

 18

Yasuhiro is talking to his coworker Martyn, who is visiting their company's office in Tokyo. Listen and circle the correct plans in Martyn's diary.

Friday	Lunch with Yasuhiro / Lunch meeting
Saturday	Baseball game with Yasuhiro / Running

49

UNIT 9 Making Invitations

3 | Conversation

  18

Practice the conversation with your partner.

Yasuhiro: Hello, Martyn. How are you?
Martyn: Very well, thank you. And you?
Yasuhiro: Couldn't be better. Actually, Yuki, Nao, and I are going out for lunch. <u>I was wondering if you would like to</u> join us.
Martyn: <u>That's very kind of you, but</u> I have to attend a lunch meeting.
Yasuhiro: <u>That's a shame. Perhaps another time</u>.
Martyn: Yes, I'd like that. Thank you for asking me.
Yasuhiro: Actually, I'm glad I ran into you, because I wanted to ask you about the weekend. Do you have any plans?
Martyn: Not yet.
Yasuhiro: Well, I'm going to watch a baseball game with some friends. <u>Would you like to come with us?</u>
Martyn: <u>Yes, I'd be happy to</u>. That sounds fun.
Yasuhiro: <u>Great. I'll email you the details later</u>.
Martyn: Thank you.

4 | Useful Expressions

Complete the expressions with words from the conversation.

Making an invitation	Accepting an invitation
F: I was wondering if you would like to have dinner? **S**: **(1)** _____ you like to go for dinner? **C**: Do you want to join us for dinner?	**F**: Yes, I'd be **(2)** _____ to. **S**: Yes, I'd love to. **C**: Yes, that sounds fun.
Refusing an invitation	**Responding**
F: That's very **(3)** _____ of you, but I'm busy. **S**: I'd love to, but I have an appointment. **C**: I'm sorry, but I have to work late.	• *If they accept:* Great. Let me give you the details. • *If they refuse:* That's a shame/too bad. Perhaps **(4)** _____ time.

5 | Speaking

Make similar conversations to the one above using the ideas in the boxes.

Lunchtime Invitation	Lunchtime Plans	Weekend Invitation
• go for a coffee • go to the park • go out for ramen • get a sandwich	• make a phone call • finish a report • go to a conference • meet a customer	• play golf • go to karaoke • visit a temple • go shopping

6 Reading

Read the article and choose the correct answers to the questions.

Taking a Guest to a Restaurant

When looking after a visitor from another country, you will probably want to take them out for dinner while they are visiting. Here are some tips to help you make sure the evening is a success.

First of all, before you do anything else, check if the visitor has any special dietary requirements. Are they vegetarian? Are they allergic to anything? Are there any foods they can't eat because of their religion? You need this information before you choose the restaurant. Forgetting to ask about this could lead to a very embarrassing evening.

Most guests enjoy the chance to try some local or traditional food, but please check with your guest before you book the restaurant. Also remember that you will need to explain the dishes to your guest, so do some research before you go out for dinner. What are the ingredients? What is special about this dish? Your guest will likely be interested to learn about your culture.

Finally, remember to help your guest. Show your guest how to eat the different dishes and explain which sauces to use. Make sure you offer to order food and drinks for your guest if they do not speak your language – and try to recommend dishes you think they will enjoy.

1. What is the purpose of this article?
   - **A.** To help people choose a good restaurant
   - **B.** To help people look after guests
   - **C.** To help people choose what to order
   - **D.** To help people learn about other cultures

2. What should hosts do before they choose a restaurant?
   - **A.** Check where it is
   - **B.** Check what food the guest can eat
   - **C.** Check the prices
   - **D.** Find somewhere special

3. Which way of helping guests is NOT mentioned?
   - **A.** Placing orders
   - **B.** Explaining when to use sauces
   - **C.** Telling guests what to say before eating
   - **D.** Showing how to eat different dishes

4. In the article, the word "local" in paragraph 3, line 1 is closest in meaning to
   - **A.** regional
   - **B.** famous
   - **C.** modern
   - **D.** delicious

UNIT 9 — Making Invitations

7 | Example Business Email

Read this **SEMI-FORMAL** email from Yasuhiro to the members of his team. What should the people who receive this email do?

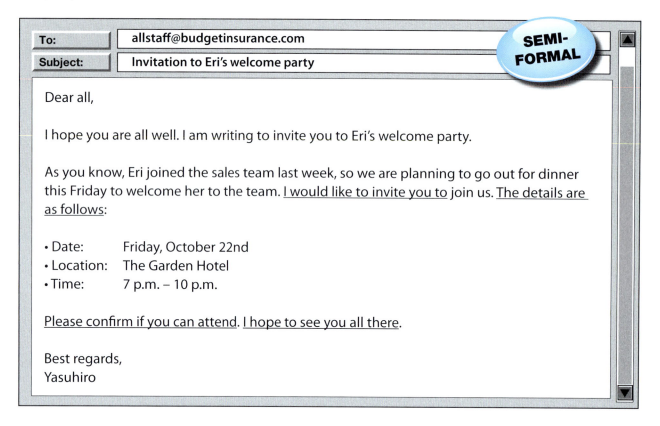

```
To:       allstaff@budgetinsurance.com
Subject:  Invitation to Eri's welcome party
```

Dear all,

I hope you are all well. I am writing to invite you to Eri's welcome party.

As you know, Eri joined the sales team last week, so we are planning to go out for dinner this Friday to welcome her to the team. I would like to invite you to join us. The details are as follows:

- Date: Friday, October 22nd
- Location: The Garden Hotel
- Time: 7 p.m. – 10 p.m.

Please confirm if you can attend. I hope to see you all there.

Best regards,
Yasuhiro

8 | Essential Email Expressions

Write **F** (formal), **S** (semi-formal), or **C** (casual) next to each expression in the chart.

Making an invitation	Introducing the details (in list form)
1. ( ) **I'd like you to** come to dinner with us.	4. ( ) Here are the details:
2. ( ) **I would like to invite you to** join us for dinner.	5. ( ) The details are as follows:
3. ( ) **I would be happy if you could** join us for dinner.	6. ( ) Please refer to the details below:
Asking for confirmation	**Referencing the event**
7. ( ) Please confirm your attendance.	10. ( ) Look forward to seeing you there.
8. ( ) Please confirm if you can attend.	11. ( ) It would be wonderful if you could attend.
9. ( ) Let me know if you can come.	12. ( ) I hope to see you there.

9 | Writing Task 1

Choose the correct expressions to complete this **CASUAL** email from Yasuhiro to a group of his university friends.

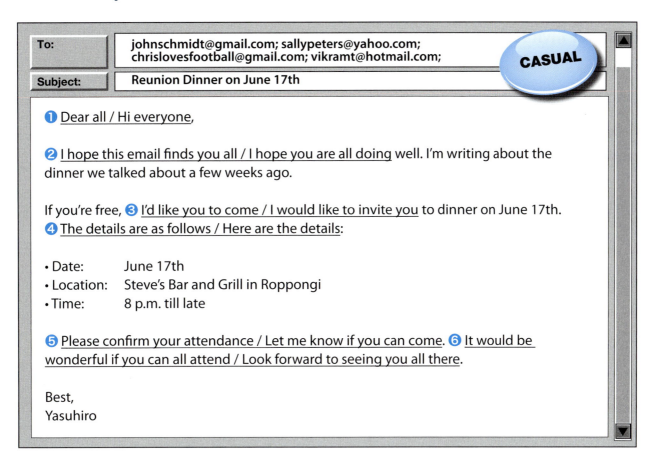

To:	johnschmidt@gmail.com; sallypeters@yahoo.com; chrislovesfootball@gmail.com; vikramt@hotmail.com;
Subject:	Reunion Dinner on June 17th

CASUAL

❶ Dear all / Hi everyone,

❷ I hope this email finds you all / I hope you are all doing well. I'm writing about the dinner we talked about a few weeks ago.

If you're free, ❸ I'd like you to come / I would like to invite you to dinner on June 17th. ❹ The details are as follows / Here are the details:

- Date: June 17th
- Location: Steve's Bar and Grill in Roppongi
- Time: 8 p.m. till late

❺ Please confirm your attendance / Let me know if you can come. ❻ It would be wonderful if you can all attend / Look forward to seeing you all there.

Best,
Yasuhiro

Business Writing Tip

Writing Group Mails

When you are writing an email to a group of people, you can mostly use the same language as when you are writing to only one person. However, you should change some key expressions by adding the word "all" or "everyone." For example:

- **Salutations** ➡ Dear *all*, / Hello *everyone*,
- **Pleasantries** ➡ I hope this email finds you *all* well. / I hope you are *all* well.
- **Purpose**   ➡ I am writing to inform you *all* about… / I am writing to thank *everyone* for…

53

UNIT 9 — Making Invitations

10 | Writing Task 2

Complete this **FORMAL** email from Yasuhiro to an important customer. Use the information below to help you.

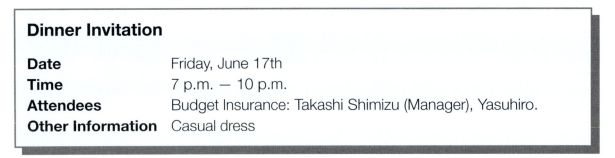

Dinner Invitation

Date	Friday, June 17th
Time	7 p.m. — 10 p.m.
Attendees	Budget Insurance: Takashi Shimizu (Manager), Yasuhiro.
Other Information	Casual dress

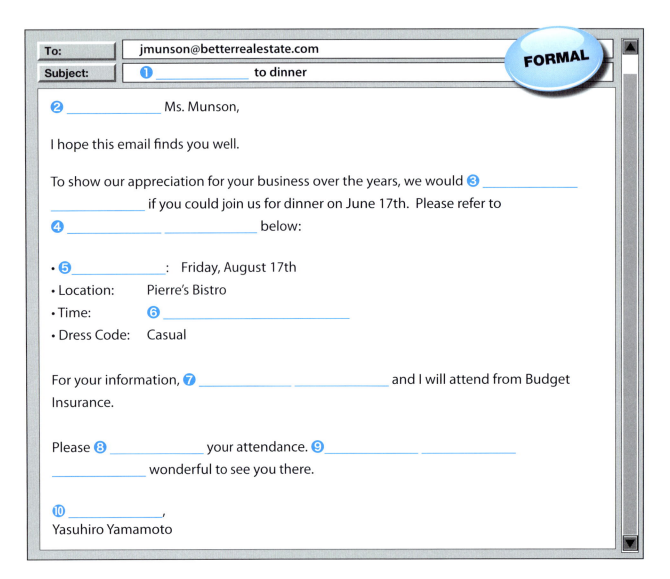

To: jmunson@betterrealestate.com
Subject: ❶ _____ to dinner

❷ _____ Ms. Munson,

I hope this email finds you well.

To show our appreciation for your business over the years, we would ❸ _____ _____ if you could join us for dinner on June 17th. Please refer to ❹ _____ _____ below:

- ❺ _____: Friday, August 17th
- Location: Pierre's Bistro
- Time: ❻ _____
- Dress Code: Casual

For your information, ❼ _____ _____ and I will attend from Budget Insurance.

Please ❽ _____ your attendance. ❾ _____ _____ _____ wonderful to see you there.

❿ _____,
Yasuhiro Yamamoto

54

UNIT 10 Making Appointments

GOAL ✓

Learn how to arrange a time for a meeting

1 Vocabulary

Match the underlined words to the meanings.

1. I'm <u>available</u> for a meeting on Monday. Are you free? (   )
2. Tuesday would <u>suit</u> me for the next meeting. (   )
3. We need to <u>schedule</u> our next team meeting. (   )
4. I received an <u>invite</u> to a conference. (   )
5. I might be busy on Monday, but let's <u>pencil in</u> a meeting. (   )

A. not busy **B.** invitation **C.** be right for
D. arrange something that may change **E.** decide the day and time of

2 Listening

 20

Keisuke is arranging a meeting with Donna. Listen and write the meeting in Keisuke's calendar.

	Mon	Tue	Wed	Thu	Fri
AM		10 to 12 Meeting with Mr. Chang			9 to 11 IT Training session
PM		2 to 4 Department meeting		3 to 5 Conference call with Brazil	

55

UNIT 10 Making Appointments

3 Conversation

Practice the conversation with your partner.

Keisuke: That was a really productive meeting.
Donna: Yes, we achieved a lot today.
Keisuke: So, shall we pencil in another meeting for next week?
Donna: Yes, that would be great. Let's try to book a two-hour meeting.
Keisuke: OK. Let me pull up my calendar. <u>What</u> days <u>would suit you best</u>?
Donna: I can't do Monday, but Tuesday and Wednesday are pretty open.
Keisuke: <u>I'm available</u> on Wednesday. <u>Would you prefer</u> morning <u>or</u> afternoon?
Donna: Actually, the morning <u>is better for me</u>. <u>Could you</u> meet at 10?
Keisuke: Yes, that's fine. <u>Shall I</u> come to your office this time?
Donna: That would be great.
Keisuke: OK. So, let's meet on Wednesday at 10 at your office. I'll send you an invite.
Donna: Thank you.

4 Useful Expressions

Complete the expressions with words from the conversation.

Asking about someone's availability	Explaining your availability
• **What** days **would** (1) _____ **you** best? • **When are you available?** • **Would you prefer** morning **or** afternoon?	• Monday **is the best** day **for me**. • **I'm free between** 2:00 **and** 4:00. • **I'm** (2) _____ on Wednesday.
Asking about specific places or times	Offering solutions
🇫: **Would it be OK to** meet on Friday? 🇸: (3) _____ **you** meet at 10? 🇨: **Can you** come to our office at 10?	🇫: **Would you like me to** find a meeting room? 🇸: (4) _____ I come to your office? 🇨: **How about** meeting at the coffee shop?

5 Speaking

Plan meetings with your classmates. How many people can you arrange to meet?

	Mon	Tue	Wed	Thu	Fri
AM					
PM					

Student A: Let's schedule a meeting for next week.
Student B: OK. When are you available?

6 Reading

Read the article and choose the correct answers to the questions.

When's the best time to schedule a meeting?

Imagine that you need to arrange a meeting with your team. It's an important meeting so you want to make sure everyone is listening. What's the best day and time for your meeting?

Some people think that Monday morning is the best time because everyone will be rested after the weekend. However, people often take days off on Mondays and Fridays so they can have a three-day weekend. So if you choose these days, it's likely that some people will not be available.

Early mornings aren't a good idea either. People may arrive late or have urgent tasks that they need to do at the start of the day – and this is especially true of Monday mornings, when staff need to check emails that arrived over the weekend.

However, the end of the day is also not a good time. People are tired and they want to go home, so they won't be able to think carefully about the topic of the meeting.

So when is the best time? Wednesday afternoon? Thursday afternoon? In fact, it's 2:30 p.m. on Tuesdays. According to a recent survey, this is the time when most people are happy to attend a meeting and listen to what you need to say.

1. According to the article, why are Mondays and Fridays bad days for meetings?
    A. Because people are not rested.
    B. Because people want to go home.
    C. Because people like to think carefully.
    D. Because some people are away.

2. What does NOT often happen on Mondays?
    A. People arrive early.
    B. People take the day off.
    C. People read emails.
    D. People do urgent tasks.

3. Why is the end of the day a bad time for a meeting?
    A. People have urgent tasks.
    B. People go home early.
    C. People need to send emails.
    D. People do not have enough energy.

4. What is likely to be the best time for a meeting?
    A. Tuesday morning
    B. Tuesday afternoon
    C. Wednesday afternoon
    D. Thursday afternoon

UNIT 10 | Making Appointments

7 | Example Business Email

Read this **SEMI-FORMAL** email from Keisuke to a senior coworker in another department. When does Keisuke want to meet?

To: dave.coleman@premiumchocolate.com
Subject: Request for appointment to discuss branding

SEMI-FORMAL

Dear Dave,

I hope all is well. When you have time, <u>I would like to meet to</u> discuss the branding strategy for our new line of Belgian chocolates.

Please <u>could you tell me your availability</u> for next week? Monday or Tuesday <u>would be convenient for me</u>, as I am hoping to finish my proposal by next Friday. <u>I could</u> set up a web conference if you're working from home.

I hope to hear from you soon.

Best regards,
Keisuke

8 | Essential Email Expressions

Write **F** (formal), **S** (semi-formal), or **C** (casual) next to each expression in the chart.

Requesting an appointment	Asking about availability
1. (　) **I would like to meet to** discuss …	4. (　) When are you free?
2. (　) **I'd like to meet to** talk about …	5. (　) Could you tell me your availability?
3. (　) **I would appreciate it if we could meet to** decide …	6. (　) Could you tell me what time would be most convenient for you?
Stating preferences for days or times	**Giving options**
7. (　) **If possible, I would prefer to** meet on Monday at 2 p.m.	10. (　) **I could** arrange a meeting room.
8. (　) Monday at 2 p.m. **would be best for me**.	11. (　) **I would be happy to** come to your office.
9. (　) Monday at 2 p.m. **would be convenient for me**.	12. (　) **It's no problem for me to** come in early.

58

9 Writing Task 1

Choose the correct expressions to complete this **CASUAL** email from Keisuke to his coworker.

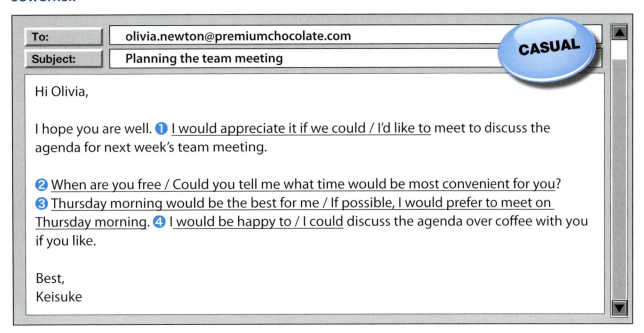

10 Writing Task 2

Put the sentences in the correct order to make a **FORMAL** email from Keisuke to an advertising company.

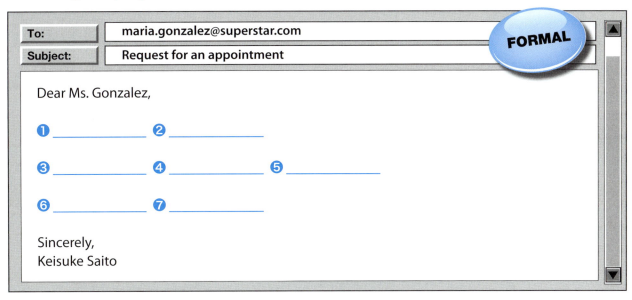

- **A.** Could you tell me what day next week would be most convenient for you?
- **B.** I would appreciate it if we could meet to discuss working with you on an advertising campaign.
- **C.** If possible, I would prefer to meet on Tuesday or Wednesday morning.
- **D.** I look forward to hearing from you.
- **E.** Please do not hesitate to ask if you have any questions.
- **F.** I would be happy to come to your office for the meeting.
- **G.** I hope this email finds you well.

UNIT 10 Making Appointments

11 | Writing Task 3

Complete this **SEMI-FORMAL** email from Keisuke to a coworker from another department.

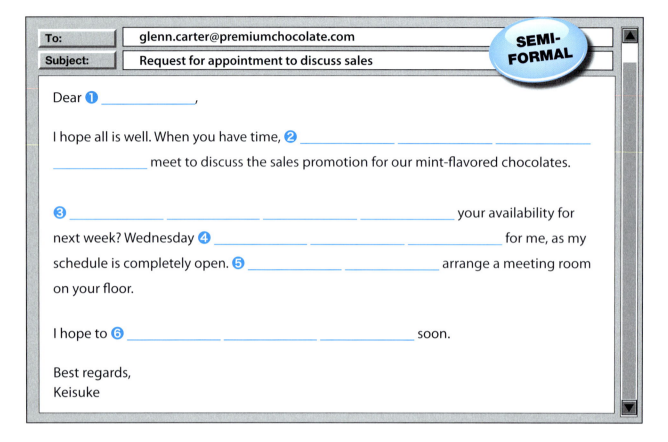

To: glenn.carter@premiumchocolate.com
Subject: Request for appointment to discuss sales

Dear ❶ _____ ,

I hope all is well. When you have time, ❷ _____ _____ _____ _____ meet to discuss the sales promotion for our mint-flavored chocolates.

❸ _____ _____ _____ _____ your availability for next week? Wednesday ❹ _____ _____ _____ for me, as my schedule is completely open. ❺ _____ _____ arrange a meeting room on your floor.

I hope to ❻ _____ _____ _____ soon.

Best regards,
Keisuke

Business Writing Tip

Contractions and Full Forms

Contractions sound casual and friendly, so you can use them when contacting friends or coworkers. Full forms are more formal, so they are better when contacting customers, senior staff or people we do not know well.

- My name**'s** Motohiro Hasebe. ➡ My name **is** Motohiro Hasebe.
- I**'d** like to meet to discuss the designs. ➡ I **would** like to meet to discuss the designs.

UNIT 11
Canceling and Rescheduling

GOAL ✓

Learn how to cancel or reschedule a meeting

1 Vocabulary

Match the underlined words to the meanings.

1. He's running late <u>due to</u> a problem with the trains. (   )
2. Can we <u>switch</u> the meeting to Thursday? (   )
3. "Are you free at 3 o'clock?" "Yes, that <u>works for</u> me." (   )
4. Mr. Smith is ill today, so we need to <u>postpone</u> the meeting. (   )
5. There's a <u>last-minute</u> change to the meeting location. (   )

   A. change **B.** because of **C.** late
   D. delay   **E.** is OK for

2 Listening 22

Chihana needs to change the time of a meeting. Listen and choose the correct answers to the questions.

1. Why does Chihana need to change the time of the meeting?
   A. She has to talk with her boss.
   B. She needs to meet a customer.
   C. She wants to meet someone for lunch.

2. When will they have the meeting?
   A. Lunchtime
   B. 4 p.m. today
   C. 10 a.m. tomorrow

61

UNIT 11   Canceling and Rescheduling

3 | Conversation

Practice the conversation with your partner.

Chihana: Teri, <u>I'm really sorry, but</u> I need to cancel our meeting this morning. <u>I have to</u> visit a customer due to a problem with their order. <u>Can we</u> postpone our meeting until later today?

Teri: Sure, but when are you available? I'm pretty busy this afternoon.

Chihana: I'm free at two or at four. Do either of those times work for you?

Teri: No, sorry. I have a team meeting at two and I'm meeting a customer at four.

Chihana: How about talking over lunch?

Teri: Sorry. I have a meeting with Bryan at lunch.

Chihana: Well, would it be possible to switch the meeting to tomorrow?

Teri: Yes, that's fine. I'm free all morning.

Chihana: Great. Let's meet in the coffee shop at 10 then. <u>Thanks for rescheduling</u> at the last minute.

Teri: No problem.

4 | Useful Expressions

Complete the expressions with words from the conversation.

Cushioning	Giving an explanation
• Unfortunately, ... • I am afraid that ... • I'm really sorry, **(1)** _____ ...	• **I need to** attend another meeting. • **I have (2)** _____ visit a customer. • **I have been asked to** give a presentation.
Requesting to cancel or reschedule	Thanking
F: **Would it be possible to** postpone our meeting? **S**: **Could we** re-arrange our meeting? **C**: **Can we** move the meeting?	**F**: I appreciate your understanding. **S**: Thank you for being so flexible. **C**: Thanks **(3)** _____ rescheduling.

5 | Speaking

Role-play conversations similar to the one above using the information below.

Conversation 1		Conversation 2	
Student A	**Student B**	**Student B**	**Student A**
• today at 2 p.m.? • today at 5 p.m.? • tomorrow at 11 a.m.?	IT training meeting free	• tomorrow at 3 p.m.? • Friday at 5 p.m.? • next Monday at 2 p.m.?	conference day off free

6 Reading

Read the article and choose the correct answers to the questions.

How to reschedule a meeting

We all need to reschedule a meeting or appointment at some point in our lives. However, there is a right and a wrong way to do it if you want to succeed in business.

The most important thing is to think about the other person. Did they make special plans to meet with you? Do they have to travel far? If the answer to either of these questions is yes, you really shouldn't reschedule as it could damage your relationship. However, if it is unavoidable, it is usually better to call first to explain and apologize verbally, then to follow up with an email. And of course, always try to give them as much notice as possible.

It's not polite to reschedule the day before the meeting and even worse to try to reschedule on the same day of the meeting. However, if you absolutely *have* to change the day or time, then you should have a really good reason (for example, a family emergency or a sudden illness). You need to apologize and reschedule the meeting for a time and place that suits them. For example, if they were originally coming to your office, you could offer to go to their office instead. You may also need to buy them lunch to thank them for making a last-minute change.

However, there are three situations when you should *never* try to reschedule a meeting: if the meeting is early in the morning the next day, if you've already rescheduled it once, or if the meeting involves multiple people. If it is early morning the following day, the other person may not get the message in time. If you have already rescheduled once, the other person may feel you are very unreliable. And if there are multiple people attending, it will be difficult to find a new time that suits everyone.

1. What is the article about?
   - **A.** Making appointments
   - **B.** Excuses for not attending meetings
   - **C.** Reserving meetings
   - **D.** Changing the time of meetings

2. What should you think about before rescheduling a meeting?
   - **A.** How far the person must travel
   - **B.** How long the meeting is
   - **C.** How important the person is
   - **D.** How important the meeting is

3. What is NOT something you should do when you reschedule the meeting at the last minute?
   - **A.** Say sorry
   - **B.** Take the other person out for a meal
   - **C.** Let the other person choose a new time
   - **D.** Send a present

4. In the article, the word "multiple" in paragraph 4, line 3 is closest in meaning to
   - **A.** double
   - **B.** several
   - **C.** international
   - **D.** important

UNIT 11 Canceling and Rescheduling

7 | Example Business Email

Read this **SEMI-FORMAL** email from Chihana to her coworker. When are they planning to meet? When does Chihana want to change the meeting to?

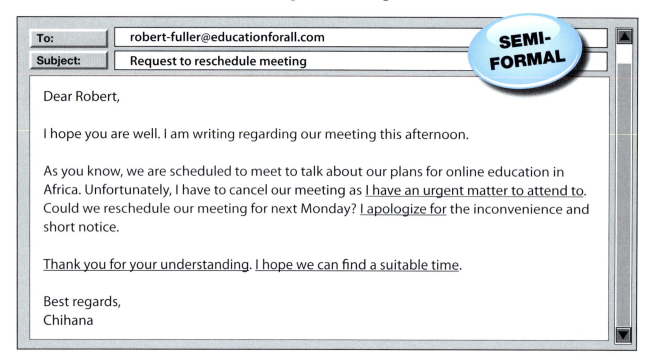

To: robert-fuller@educationforall.com
Subject: Request to reschedule meeting

Dear Robert,

I hope you are well. I am writing regarding our meeting this afternoon.

As you know, we are scheduled to meet to talk about our plans for online education in Africa. Unfortunately, I have to cancel our meeting as I have an urgent matter to attend to. Could we reschedule our meeting for next Monday? I apologize for the inconvenience and short notice.

Thank you for your understanding. I hope we can find a suitable time.

Best regards,
Chihana

8 | Essential Email Expressions

Write **F** (formal), **S** (semi-formal), or **C** (casual) next to each expression in the chart.

Giving vague reasons	Apologizing
1. ( ) I have to cancel our meeting **as I have an urgent matter to attend to.**	4. ( ) **Please accept my apologies for** the inconvenience.
2. ( ) I have to cancel our meeting **due to circumstances beyond our control.**	5. ( ) **I'm sorry for** the inconvenience.
3. ( ) I have to cancel our meeting **because something came up.**	6. ( ) **I apologize for** the inconvenience.
Thanking after bad news	**Referencing the next meeting**
7. ( ) Thank you for your understanding.	10. ( ) I hope we can find a convenient time.
8. ( ) Thanks for understanding.	11. ( ) I hope we can find a time that works for both of us.
9. ( ) Thank you for your kind understanding.	12. ( ) Hope we can make this work.

9 | Writing Task 1

Choose the correct expressions to complete this **CASUAL** email from Chihana to her coworker.

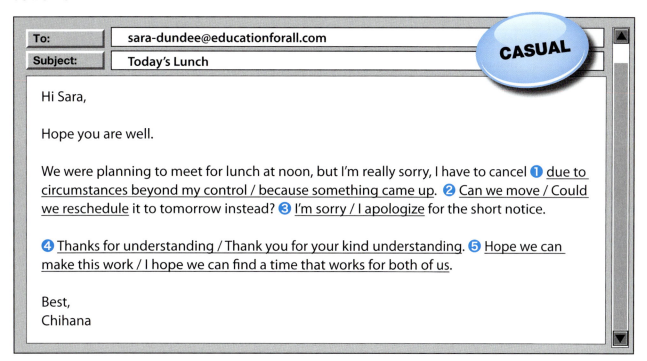

10 | Writing Task 2

Complete this **FORMAL** email from Chihana to a customer.

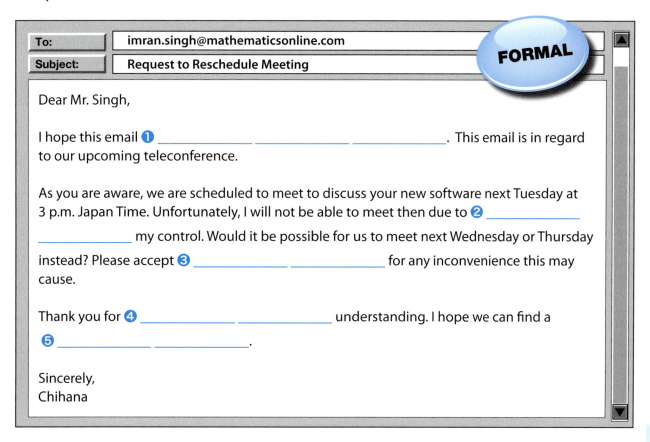

65

UNIT 11   **Canceling and Rescheduling**

11 | *Writing Task 3*

Put the sentences in the correct order to make a **SEMI-FORMAL** email from Chihana to her senior coworker.

To:	joe-gomez@educationforall.com
Subject:	Request to Reschedule Appointment

SEMI-FORMAL

Dear Joe,

(   ) I apologize for the short notice.

(   ) As you know, we agreed to meet to discuss the budget for next year.

(   ) Could we reschedule our meeting for next week?

(   ) Thank you for your understanding.

(   ) I hope we can find a convenient time.

(   ) I am writing in regard to our appointment on Thursday.

(   ) Unfortunately, I have an urgent matter to attend to, so I will not be able to meet on Thursday.

(1) I hope you are well.

Best regards,
Chihana

Business Writing Tip

Using "I" and "We"

In emails and phone calls, you need to decide whether to talk about "I" or "We" (your company). Use "I" to sound more personal and talk about your own feelings or actions. Use "we" to sound more formal and talk about company decisions or actions.

- **I** would like to express **my** appreciation for your help.
- **We** would like to express **our** appreciation for your order.

66

UNIT 12 Describing Locations

GOAL ✓

Learn how to ask for and give directions

1 Vocabulary

Match the underlined words to the meanings.

1. If you need the restroom, it's <u>straight down</u> here. (   )
2. The cafe is at the end of this <u>hallway</u>. (   )
3. The IT Department? Just <u>go through</u> that door. (   )
4. Our office is <u>across from</u> the park. We can see it from the windows. (   )
5. Turn right when you <u>reach</u> a yellow door. (   )

    A. open and walk through   **B.** arrive at   **C.** along

    D. opposite   **E.** a long passage inside a buidling

2 Listening

 24

Midori is giving directions to a visitor to her office. Listen and match the places to the locations on the map.

1. the restrooms (   )   2. a vending machine (   )   3. the coffee shop (   )

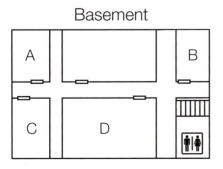

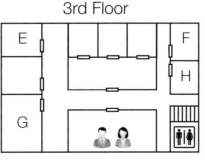

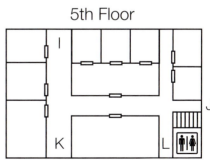

UNIT 12 — Describing Locations

3 | Conversation

  24

Practice the conversation with your partner.

Jason: Excuse me. <u>Could you tell me the way to</u> the restroom, <u>please</u>?

Midori: Certainly. <u>Go through that door and turn left</u>. Then <u>go straight down to the end of the hallway</u> and turn right. <u>It's on the left side</u>.

Jason: Left and then right at the end of the hallway.

Midori: That's right.

Jason: And <u>is there</u> a drink vending machine <u>in this building</u>?

Midori: Yes, <u>there's one on the fifth floor</u>. <u>It's on your left</u> when you get out of the elevator. There's a coffee shop downstairs too.

Jason: Really?

Midori: Yes, <u>it's in the basement</u>. If you take the elevator, you'll see a drugstore. The coffee shop <u>is just behind</u> the drugstore.

4 | Useful Expressions

Complete the expressions with words from the conversation.

Asking for directions	Saying where a place is
• **Could you tell me the (1)** _____ **to** the restroom, please? • **Is there a** vending machine **near here?** • **Where is** the elevator?	• It's **on** the first floor. • It's **in** the lobby. • It's **(2)** _____ the basement.
Giving directions	Describing locations
• **Go (3)** _____ **down** the hallway. • **Go past** the kitchen. • **Take a right** at the water cooler.	• It's **near / next** to the elevator. • It's **to the left / to the right** of the restroom. • It's **just (4)** _____ the drugstore.

5 | Speaking

Take turns asking each other for directions to these places on the map.

the photocopier • the elevator • Meeting Room 6 • the kitchen • the Accounts Department

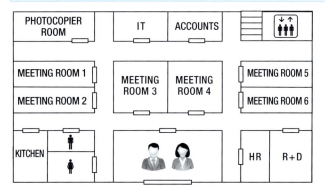

Student A: Excuse me. Could you tell me the way to Meeting Room 6?

Student B: Sure. Go …

6 Reading

Read the article and choose the correct answers to the questions.

Apple's New "Spaceship Campus"

Apple has spent years building a new high-tech headquarters in California at a cost of almost $5 billion. So what's it like inside?

First of all, it's huge – and it has to be, because this large, circular building will provide space for over 12,000 members of staff. The round design was chosen because it means there are lots of windows and therefore lots of light. There are also only four floors, so that staff don't often need to use the elevators. Each department is on a different floor and the offices have an open-plan layout. This means that staff in each department do not have an assigned desk and can sit next to the people that they need to work with on that day.

There are also lots of great facilities for staff. There is a large fitness center, seven cafés, and a 1,000-seat auditorium, which will be used for presentations and product launches. There are also bikes for staff to use to cycle around the campus.

It's also a very environmentally friendly building. The roof is covered in solar panels and the building will use recycled water. In fact, Steve Jobs, the former CEO of Apple, wanted the building to feel more like a nature park than an office, so the building is in the middle of a large park with over 7,000 trees. Staff can walk around the park when they take a break.

1. What is the main purpose of the article?
   - **A.** To explain the cost of the new office
   - **B.** To explain the features of the new office
   - **C.** To explain the size of the new office
   - **D.** To explain the address of the new office

2. According to the article, why did Apple use a circular design?
   - **A.** Because it has a lot of space
   - **B.** Because it is very high tech
   - **C.** Because it provides a lot of light
   - **D.** Because it is environmentally friendly

3. What facility is NOT included in the new office?
   - **A.** A theater
   - **B.** A gym
   - **C.** A doctor's office
   - **D.** A place to eat

4. How many employees work at the office?
   - **A.** 1,000
   - **B.** 7,000
   - **C.** 12,000
   - **D.** 5,000

UNIT 12 Describing Locations

7 Example Business Email

Read this **SEMI-FORMAL** email from Midori to a supplier who will visit her office. What file has she attached to this email?

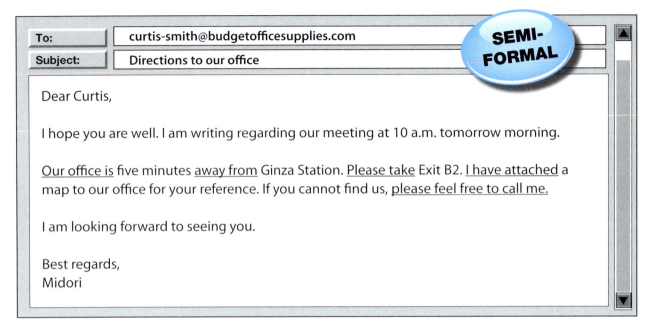

To: curtis-smith@budgetofficesupplies.com
Subject: Directions to our office

SEMI-FORMAL

Dear Curtis,

I hope you are well. I am writing regarding our meeting at 10 a.m. tomorrow morning.

<u>Our office is</u> five minutes <u>away from</u> Ginza Station. <u>Please take</u> Exit B2. <u>I have attached</u> a map to our office for your reference. If you cannot find us, <u>please feel free to call me.</u>

I am looking forward to seeing you.

Best regards,
Midori

8 Essential Email Expressions

Write **F** (formal), **S** (semi-formal), or **C** (casual) next to each expression in the chart.

Explaining the location	Giving directions
1. ( ) **Our office is located** about five minutes **from**…	4. ( ) **When you arrive, please leave the station at** Exit A5.
2. ( ) **We are** 5 minutes on foot **from**…	5. ( ) **Please take** Exit A5.
3. ( ) **Our office is** five minutes **away from**…	6. ( ) **Take** Exit A5.
Referencing attachments	Offering help
7. ( ) **I have attached** a map to our office for your reference.	10. ( ) If you get lost, **please give me a call**.
8. ( ) **Please find attached** a map for your reference.	11. ( ) If you cannot find us, **please feel free to call me**.
9. ( ) **Here is** a map to our office.	12. ( ) If you have any trouble, **please do not hesitate to call**.

70

9 Writing Task 1

Choose the correct expressions to complete this **CASUAL** email from Midori to her friend.

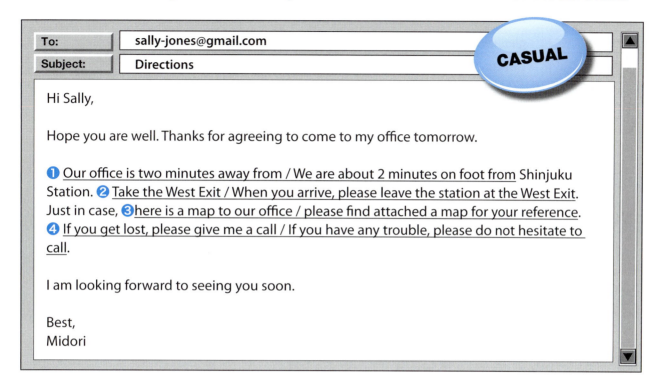

10 Writing Task 2

Complete this **FORMAL** email from Midori to a customer.

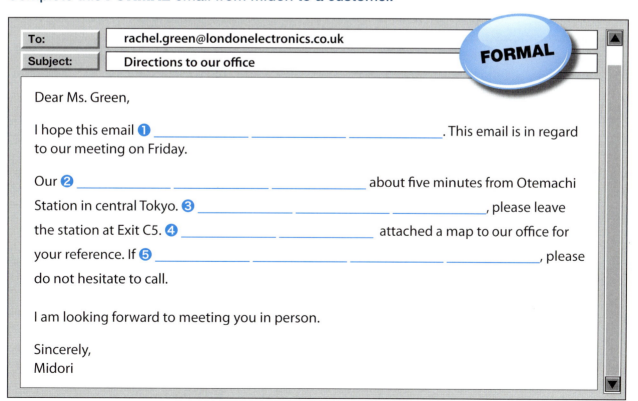

UNIT 12 | Describing Locations

11 | Writing Task 3

Complete this **SEMI-FORMAL** email from Midori to a coworker from an overseas branch.

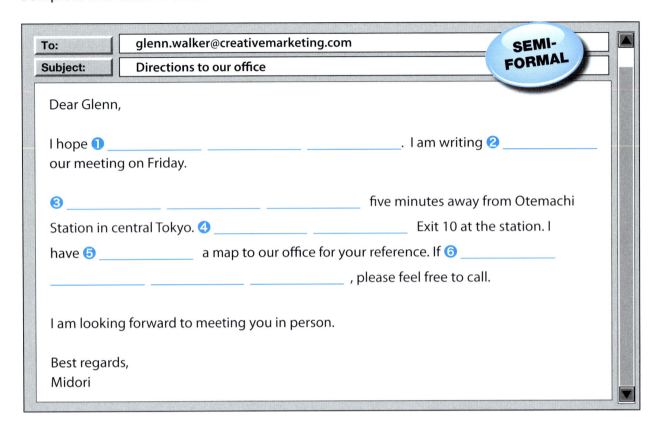

To: glenn.walker@creativemarketing.com
Subject: Directions to our office

SEMI-FORMAL

Dear Glenn,

I hope ❶ _____ _____ _____. I am writing ❷ _____ our meeting on Friday.

❸ _____ _____ _____ five minutes away from Otemachi Station in central Tokyo. ❹ _____ _____ Exit 10 at the station. I have ❺ _____ a map to our office for your reference. If ❻ _____ _____ _____ _____, please feel free to call.

I am looking forward to meeting you in person.

Best regards,
Midori

Business Writing Tip

Numbers

The use of numbers is very important when writing emails, as how you use them can change the impression of your email. For lower numbers, it is more formal to write the words. For higher numbers, we almost always use numbers.

- **Formal / Semi-Formal** ➡ Two weeks, twelve months, one hundred units
- **Casual** ➡ 2 weeks, 12 months, 100 units
- **All Emails** ➡ 101 (not one hundred and one)

However, you should always use numbers with units (for example, 100 cm, $300).

UNIT 13 Looking after a Visitor

GOAL ✓

Learn how to look after a visitor to your office, make small talk, and send a follow-up email

1 Vocabulary

Match the underlined words to the meanings.

1. Please take a seat and <u>make yourself comfortable</u>. (   )
2. The meeting will start <u>shortly</u>. (   )
3. Would you <u>care for</u> some water? (   )
4. I need to get some documents. I'll <u>be right back</u>. (   )
5. I will <u>escort</u> you to the meeting room. (   )

    A. return quickly   **B.** in a few minutes   **C.** like
    D. take   **E.** relax

2 Listening

 26

Shinya is greeting a visitor to his company. Listen and choose the correct visitor.

(1) • **Name:** John Lawson • **Works in:** Norway • **Drinks:** Tea	(2) • **Name:** Lars Eriksen • **Works in:** Denmark • **Drinks:** Tea
(3) • **Name:** Erik Larsen • **Works in:** Sweden • **Drinks:** Coffee	(4) • **Name:** Greg Carlsen • **Works in:** Holland • **Drinks:** Coffee

UNIT 13 Looking after a Visitor

3 Conversation

  26

Practice the conversation with your partner.

Shinya: Hello. Are you Mr. Larsen?
Mr. Larsen: Yes, that's right.
Shinya: My name's Shinya Ogawa. It's a pleasure to meet you.
Mr. Larsen: It's nice to meet you, too.
Shinya: <u>Let me escort you to</u> the meeting room. Please follow me.
Mr. Larsen: Thank you.
Shinya: You're based in Stockholm, aren't you?
Mr. Larsen: Yes, that's right.
Shinya: <u>How's the weather in</u> Stockholm at the moment?
Mr. Larsen: It's pretty hot and sunny, but not as humid as Tokyo.
Shinya: Yes, it's very humid here. OK. This is the meeting room. Please have a seat.
Mr. Larsen: Thank you.
Shinya: Mr. Kaneda <u>will be with you shortly</u>. <u>Would you care for</u> something to drink?
Mr. Larsen: Could I have a coffee, please?
Shinya: Certainly. Please make yourself comfortable. I'll be right back with your coffee.

4 Useful Expressions

Complete the expressions with words from the conversation.

Looking after the visitor	Making small talk
• Let me (1) _____ you to the meeting room. • The meeting room **is this way.** • **May I take** your coat?	• **How was** your flight/journey/weekend? • **Have you been to** Tokyo **before**? • (2) _____ the weather in Stockholm at the moment?
Asking the visitor to wait	**Offering food or drink**
• Mr. Kaneda **will be with you** (3) _____. • **Please wait here** a moment. • **She'll be with you in** a moment.	F: **Would you (4) _____ for** something to drink? S: **Could I get you** something to eat? C: **Can I get you** a drink?

5 Speaking

Work in pairs. Make conversations similar to the one above for these visitors.

| Lisa Jones from Sydney | Miguel Sanchez from Mexico City | Mei Ling Zhao from Beijing |

6 Reading

Read the article and choose the correct answers to the questions.

To give or not to give

When you visit customers, suppliers, or coworkers in other countries, you may want to give a small gift to thank the other people for looking after you. However, it's important to be aware of different gift-giving customs around the world so that you do not accidentally give the wrong gift. – [1] –

First of all, check that gift giving is appropriate for employees of the company you are working with. Most companies do not allow employees to receive expensive gifts, and some companies do not allow their employees to receive gifts at all. – [2] –

If gift giving is allowed, be careful about what gift you give. For example, in China, giving a clock or a watch as a present suggests death will come to the receiver soon. Similarly, giving a comb in Japan is considered bad luck as the Japanese word for comb, "kushi," means suffering and death. In Sweden, you should never give soap as a present, as people believe that it may wash your friendship away. – [3] –

Numbers are also important when giving gifts. In Europe, North America and some other countries, the number 13 is considered extremely unlucky for religious reasons. – [4] –

So does this mean you should avoid giving gifts? No, but you should always research a country's gift-giving customs before you buy anything.

1. What is the purpose of the article?
   A. To provide ideas for gift giving
   B. To give people advice about gift giving
   C. To explain gift-giving customs in the U.S.
   D. To tell people not to give gifts

2. What does the writer say is a reason for giving gifts?
   A. To greet someone
   B. To share your customs
   C. To say thank you
   D. To look after people

3. What would likely be the safest gift for a Swedish customer?
   A. A box of 13 cakes
   B. A very expensive clock
   C. A box of soaps
   D. Four cups

4. In which of the following positions marked [1], [2], [3] and [4] does the following sentence best belong? "If you're not sure about the policy, you should check with the person you wish to buy a gift for."
   A. [1]
   B. [2]
   C. [3]
   D. [4]

UNIT 13 Looking after a Visitor

7 Example Business Email

Read this **SEMI-FORMAL** email from Shinya to a supplier that he visited in New York. Why is he saying thank you to the supplier?

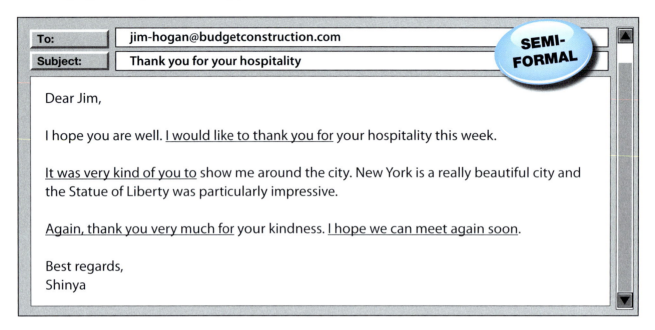

8 Essential Email Expressions

Write **F** (formal), **S** (semi-formal), or **C** (casual) next to each expression in the chart.

Thanking someone for their help	Saying what they did
1. ( ) **I would like to express my appreciation for** your hospitality.	4. ( ) **I really appreciate how you** showed me around.
2. ( ) **Thanks so much for** looking after me.	5. ( ) **It was very kind of you to** show we around.
3. ( ) **I would like to thank you for** your hospitality.	6. ( ) **It was good of you to** show me around.
Repeating your thanks	**Closing pleasantry**
7. ( ) **Again, thank you for** looking after me.	10. ( ) Hope to see you again soon.
8. ( ) **Once again, I am very grateful for** your kindness.	11. ( ) I hope we can meet again soon.
9. ( ) **Thanks again!**	12. ( ) I look forward to meeting with you again soon.

76

9 | Writing Task 1

Choose the correct expressions to complete this **CASUAL** email from Shinya to his friend.

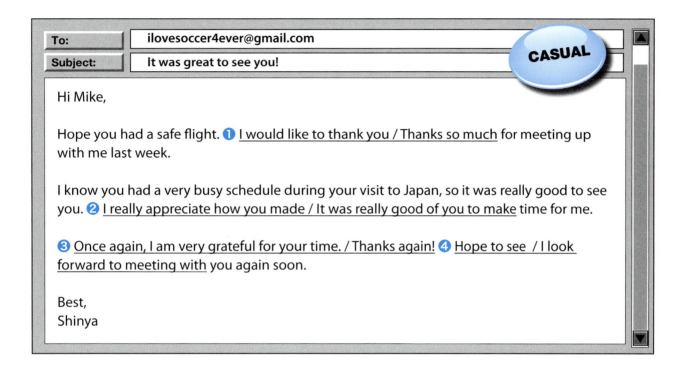

To: ilovesoccer4ever@gmail.com
Subject: It was great to see you!

Hi Mike,

Hope you had a safe flight. ❶ I would like to thank you / Thanks so much for meeting up with me last week.

I know you had a very busy schedule during your visit to Japan, so it was really good to see you. ❷ I really appreciate how you made / It was really good of you to make time for me.

❸ Once again, I am very grateful for your time. / Thanks again! ❹ Hope to see / I look forward to meeting with you again soon.

Best,
Shinya

10 | Writing Task 2

Complete this **FORMAL** email from Shinya to a customer.

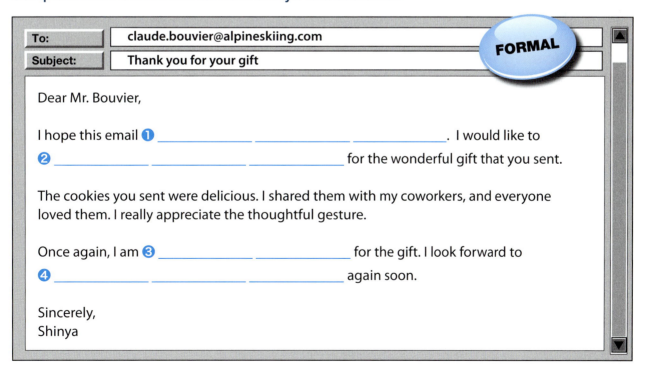

To: claude.bouvier@alpineskiing.com
Subject: Thank you for your gift

Dear Mr. Bouvier,

I hope this email ❶ _____ _____ _____. I would like to ❷ _____ _____ _____ for the wonderful gift that you sent.

The cookies you sent were delicious. I shared them with my coworkers, and everyone loved them. I really appreciate the thoughtful gesture.

Once again, I am ❸ _____ _____ for the gift. I look forward to ❹ _____ _____ _____ again soon.

Sincerely,
Shinya

UNIT 13 | Looking after a Visitor

11 | Writing Task 3

Complete this **SEMI-FORMAL** email from Shinya to a supplier from the U.S.

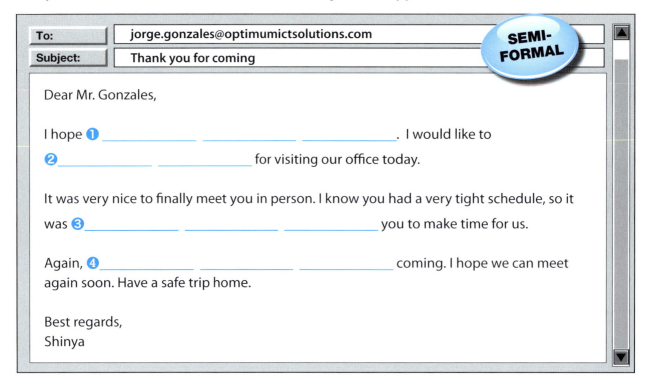

To: jorge.gonzales@optimumictsolutions.com
Subject: Thank you for coming

Dear Mr. Gonzales,

I hope ❶ _____ _____ _____. I would like to
❷ _____ _____ for visiting our office today.

It was very nice to finally meet you in person. I know you had a very tight schedule, so it was ❸ _____ _____ _____ you to make time for us.

Again, ❹ _____ _____ _____ coming. I hope we can meet again soon. Have a safe trip home.

Best regards,
Shinya

Business Writing Tip

Closing Pleasantries

You should try to end your email with a friendly comment that looks to the future. Use "I look forward to" to talk about things that have already been decided and use "I hope" for things that you want to happen. Here are some examples:

- **To a supplier** ➡ *I look forward to receiving your estimate.*
  (= You expect to get their estimate soon.)
- **To a customer** ➡ *I look forward to seeing you at the meeting.*
  (= You expect to see them at the meeting, because the details of the meeting have been agreed.)
- **To a customer** ➡ *I hope to see you at the exhibition.*
  (= You want to meet them, but they haven't agreed to come yet.)

Making a Phone Call

GOAL ✓

Learn how to make a phone call to another company and send a follow-up email

1 Vocabulary

Match the underlined words to the meanings.

1. Can you put me through to John Young, please? (   )
2. She's on another line at the moment. (   )
3. Please call me back tonight. (   )
4. Please hold the line while I look for the document. (   )
5. She's not here today. Would you like to leave a message? (   )

    A. wait (during a phone call)   **B.** tell me information to give to another person
    C. return my call   **D.** on a call with another person   **E.** connect me

2 Listening

 28

Haruko is making a phone call. Listen and choose the correct answers to the questions.

1. Who does Haruko want to speak to?
   A. Mr. Kobayashi   **B.** Doug Peterson   **C.** Amy Carter

2. Where is this person that Haruko wants to speak to?
   A. Having lunch   **B.** Talking on the phone   **C.** In a meeting

3. What does Haruko want the person she is speaking to do?
   A. Ask someone to email her
   B. Ask someone to call her
   C. Send her something

UNIT 14 Making a Phone Call

3 | Conversation

  28

Practice the conversation with your partner.

Doug: Hello, West Coast Logistics. Doug Peterson speaking.

Haruko: <u>Hello. This is</u> Haruko Kobayashi from Tokyo Shipping. <u>Could I speak to</u> Amy Carter, please?

Doug: Sure. I'll put you through. Please hold the line. Actually, I'm afraid she's on another line.

Haruko: Well, I want to ask about delivery times to Tokyo. <u>Is there anyone else I could speak to?</u>

Doug: Amy's the best person to talk to. She deals with all of our clients in Asia.

Haruko: In that case, could I leave a message? <u>Could you ask her to</u> call me when she's free?

Doug: Sure. Can I take your name again, please?

Haruko: Yes, it's Haruko Kobayashi from Tokyo Shipping.

Doug: Does she have your number?

Haruko: Yes, she does. It's in my email signature.

Doug: OK. I'll ask her to call you when she gets back.

4 | Useful Expressions

Complete the expressions with words from the conversation.

Starting a phone call	Asking for the right person
F: Good morning. My name is Emi Mori **and I'm calling from** SDC. **S: Hello. This is** Emi Mori 　(1) _____ SDC. **C: Hi. This is** Emi **from** SDC.	**F: Is it possible to speak to** the person in charge of accounts? **S: Could I speak to** Amy Carter? **C: Can I speak to** someone in IT?
Finding someone else to talk to	Asking for other help
• I wonder if you can help me then. • Is there (2) _____ else I could speak to? • **In that case, can I speak to** Bill Jones?	• Do you (3) _____ when he will be back? • **Could you ask him to** call me back? • **Could I leave a message**?

5 | Speaking

Make conversations similar to the one above for these situations.

Caller	Nao Fujita, Sony	Kaoru Yamazaki, Canon
Calling for	(Mr.) Leon Rogers	(Mrs.) Helen Braun
Person answering the phone	Alex Sanderson, Google	Robin Reeves, IBM
Location of person	Leon is in a meeting	Helen is at a conference

6 Reading

Read the article and choose the correct answers to the questions.

LINE

More than 70 million people in Japan use the social networking app LINE to send messages and share photographs, but did you know that it was created to allow people to communicate in a disaster?

When the Tohoku earthquake struck in 2011, it didn't only destroy buildings, roads and railways. It also damaged large parts of the phone network, meaning that people could not contact their relatives.

Three employees at NHN Japan (a subsidiary of a South Korean internet company) wanted to do something to solve this problem, so they came up with an idea: an app that would allow people to send messages to each other and make phone calls over the internet. Their app, LINE, provided an essential communication tool for the victims of the earthquake, but it was also hugely popular all over Japan. Within a year, it had become popular in other countries too, with over 50 million users around the world. After 18 months, it had 100 million. After another six months, it had 200 million.

Today, LINE is used by over 700 million people around the world, but the company has not forgotten the reason why it was created. LINE has sold "stickers" (special pictures that users can send to each other) to raise money for the people affected by earthquakes. They have also produced information to tell people what to do in an emergency.

1. What is the article about?
   A. The history of LINE
   B. The users of LINE
   C. The main features of LINE
   D. The stickers made by LINE

2. According to the article, why was LINE created?
   A. To warn people about earthquakes
   B. To sell stickers
   C. To help people talk after a disaster
   D. To allow people to share photographs

3. How many LINE users were there worldwide two years after it was created?
   A. 50 million   B. 100 million   C. 200 million   D. 700 million

4. In the article, the word "raise" in paragraph 4, line 3 is closest in meaning to
   A. make   B. increase   C. lift   D. introduce

81

UNIT 14 Making a Phone Call

7 | Example Business Email

Read this **SEMI-FORMAL** email from Haruko to Jason, a representative of her company's cloud storage provider. What should Jason do next?

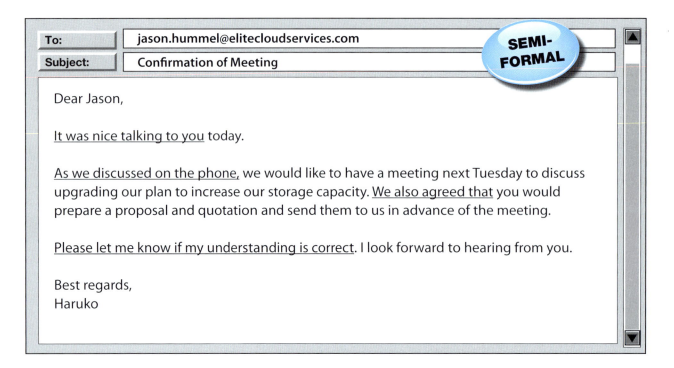

To: jason.hummel@elitecloudservices.com
Subject: Confirmation of Meeting

SEMI-FORMAL

Dear Jason,

It was nice talking to you today.

As we discussed on the phone, we would like to have a meeting next Tuesday to discuss upgrading our plan to increase our storage capacity. We also agreed that you would prepare a proposal and quotation and send them to us in advance of the meeting.

Please let me know if my understanding is correct. I look forward to hearing from you.

Best regards,
Haruko

8 | Essential Email Expressions

Write **F** (formal), **S** (semi-formal), or **C** (casual) next to each expression in the chart.

Referencing the phone call	Referring to content of the phone call
1. ( ) **Thank you for speaking with me** earlier.	4. ( ) **As we discussed on the phone,** ...
2. ( ) **It was nice talking to you** today.	5. ( ) **Following on from our conversation,** ...
3. ( ) **Good talking with you** this morning.	6. ( ) **As we said,** ...
Giving more details	**Checking understanding**
7. ( ) **It was also agreed that**...	10. ( ) **Please could you confirm** if my understanding is correct?
8. ( ) **We also agreed that**...	11. ( ) **Please let me know** if my understanding is correct.
9. ( ) **We also said that**...	12. ( ) **Is my understanding correct?**

82

9 | Writing Task 1

Choose the correct expressions to complete this **CASUAL** email from Haruko to her teammate.

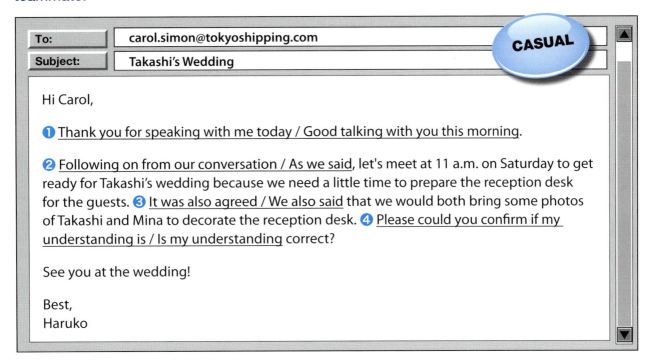

10 | Writing Task 2

Complete this **FORMAL** email from Haruko to her customer in the United States.

83

UNIT 14   **Making a Phone Call**

11 | *Writing Task 3*

Complete this **SEMI-FORMAL** email from Haruko to her customer in Sweden.

To: inga-neilson@swedesvegetabletrading.com

Subject: Confirmation of shipping schedule

SEMI-FORMAL

Dear Inga,

It was ❶ _____ _____ _____ you today.

❷ _____ _____ _____ _____ _____ phone,
your delivery is scheduled to arrive one day ahead of schedule, due to favorable winds
in the Atlantic Ocean. ❸ _____ _____ _____ that I would
notify you if there were any changes to the schedule. ❹ _____ _____
_____ _____ _____ my understanding is correct.

If you have any questions, please feel free to ask. I hope to talk with you again soon.

Best regards,
Haruko

Business Writing Tip

Introducing the Topic of your Email

You should usually explain the topic for your email at the start. This will help
the reader understand why you are writing.

F ➡ **I am writing in regard to / in reference to** your new product range.
S ➡ **I am writing regarding / concerning** this year's recruitment strategy.
C ➡ **I'm writing about** next week's meeting.

When speaking on the telephone, change the word "writing" to "calling":

• **I am calling in regard to** your new product range.

84

UNIT 15
Taking Messages

GOAL ✓

Learn how to take a message from a caller and send an email about the message

1 Vocabulary

Match the underlined words to the meanings.

1. She's just stepped out for a moment.   (   )
2. If you want to call me, my extension is 432.   (   )
3. Please ask her to get back to me before 5 o'clock?   (   )
4. Please call me back ASAP. It's urgent.   (   )
5. I'll be sure to tell him.   (   )

    A. return my call   **B.** be certain to   **C.** as soon as possible
    D. gone out   **E.** phone number inside a big company

2 Listening

 30

Yuji is taking a message for his coworker, Carla. Listen and complete his memo.

To	Carla Alvarez
Caller	
Company	
Phone number	
Message	

85

UNIT 15 Taking Messages

3 | Conversation

  30

Practice the conversation with your partner.

Yuji: Hello, Red Communications. Yuji Hoshino speaking.

Stephan: Hello. Could I speak to Carla Alvarez, please?

Yuji: I'm sorry, but <u>she's just stepped out</u> for a moment. <u>Would you like to</u> leave a message?

Stephan: Yes, could you ask her to call Stephan ASAP? It's about tomorrow's meeting.

Yuji: Certainly. Let me write that down. <u>May I take your</u> name, please?

Stephan: Yes, it's Stephan Banner from RGB Computers.

Yuji: <u>Could you spell</u> your name for me, <u>please</u>?

Stephan: Sure. Stephan is S-T-E-P-H-A-N and Banner is B-A-N-N-E-R.

Yuji: Thank you. And <u>could I have</u> your phone number, <u>please?</u>

Stephan: Yes, it's 010-583-9841 extension 682.

Yuji: <u>May I confirm that?</u> It's 010-583-9814 extension 682. Is that correct?

Stephan: No, it's 9841.

Yuji: Sorry. 9841. Thank you. And <u>let me confirm your message</u>. You want her to get back to you as soon as possible about tomorrow's meeting. Is that correct?

Stephan: Yes, that's right.

Yuji: OK. I'll be sure to give her your message.

4 | Useful Expressions

Complete the expressions with words from the conversation.

Saying people are not available	Offering help
• I'm afraid **he's not available** right now. • Unfortunately, **she's out of the office** today. • (1) _____ _____, but she's just stepped out…	• Would (2) _____ _____ to leave a message? • **May I** take a message? • **Would you like her to** call you back?
Asking for details	Checking information
• (3) _____ _____ _____ your name, please? • **Can I take** your company name, please? • **Could I have** your phone number, please?	• Could you (4) _____ your name, please? • **Could I check that? Did you say** 9814? • **Let me confirm your message.** You want her to call your cell phone. **Is that correct?**

5 | Speaking

Role-play a telephone conversation. Use the caller information below.

• **Caller's name:** Helena Miller
• **Caller's phone no.:** 030-5318-7642
You want to speak to John Brown. You need to cancel tomorrow's meeting.

• **Caller's name:** Donny James
• **Caller's phone no.:** 060-4433-1839
You want to speak to Mandy Jackson. You want her to send you a catalog.

86

6 Reading

Read the article and choose the correct answers to the questions.

When to call and when to email

Sending email is easy. You can type your message, click "send," and feel satisfied that you achieved something. However, email is not always the best way to communicate. In fact, many companies believe that their employees use email too often and that a phone call can often be more effective.

One reason that phone calls are better is because they produce quicker results. If you need to ask questions, discuss something, or make a decision, you can do all of that in a short phone call. It might seem quicker to write an email to start a discussion, but it may take days of sending emails back and forth before the conversation is finished.

Another advantage of phone calls is that they are more personal. In fact, talking on the phone can help you to maintain a good relationship with the other person, whereas emails can sometimes feel impersonal. Phone calls are also less likely to cause misunderstanding, because it's easy to interrupt and ask a question if you don't understand.

However, one good reason to send an email is when you need a written record of the conversation. This is important when you need to make sure that everyone has the same understanding about decisions or agreements.

1. What is being discussed in the article?
   A. Choosing how to communicate
   B. Facts about how people communicate
   C. How to make a good phone call
   D. Companies that don't use email

2. Which of the following is NOT given as an advantage of phone calls?
   A. People make quicker decisions
   B. People understand each other
   C. People get on well together
   D. People feel satisfied with work

3. What is suggested about emails?
   A. It can take a long time to write one.
   B. They can cause misunderstandings.
   C. They are not always received.
   D. They can be sent to the wrong person.

4. In the article, the word "record" in paragraph 4, line 1 is closest in meaning to
   A. audio
   B. achievement
   C. note
   D. resume

87

UNIT 15 Taking Messages

7 Example Business Email

Read this **SEMI-FORMAL** email from Yuji to his coworker about a phone call he received. What should John do next?

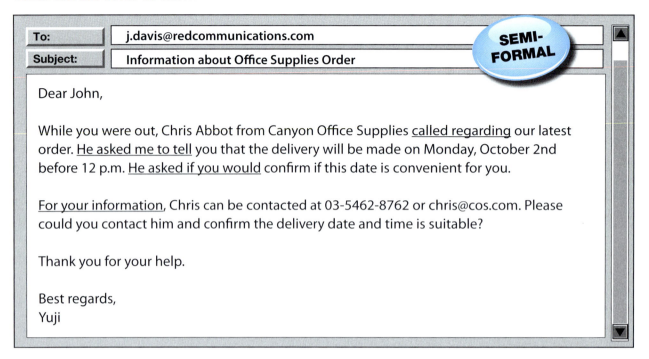

8 Essential Email Expressions

Write **F** (formal), **S** (semi-formal), or **C** (casual) next to each expression in the chart.

Explaining the topic	Passing on information
1. ( ) Chris Abbot from Canyon Office Supplies **called regarding** …	4. ( ) **He/She asked me to tell** you that…
	5. ( ) **He/She said that**…
2. ( ) Chris Abbot from Canyon Office Supplies **called in regard to** …	6. ( ) **He/She asked me to inform** you that…
3. ( ) Chris from Canyon Office Supplies **called about** …	
Passing on requests	**Giving additional information**
7. ( ) **He/She asked if you would** confirm the date.	10. ( ) **For your information**, …
	11. ( ) **For your reference**, …
8. ( ) **He/She would like you to** confirm the date.	12. ( ) **FYI**, …
9. ( ) **He/She wants you to** confirm the date.	

9 Writing Task 1

Choose the correct words and expressions to complete this **FORMAL** email from Yuji to the head of his department.

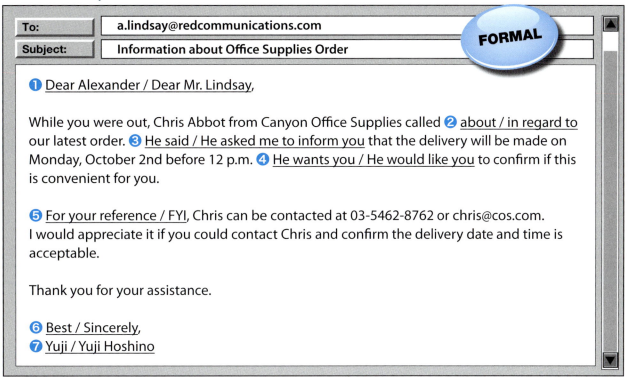

10 Writing Task 2

Choose the correct words and expressions to complete this **CASUAL** email from Yuji to a coworker.

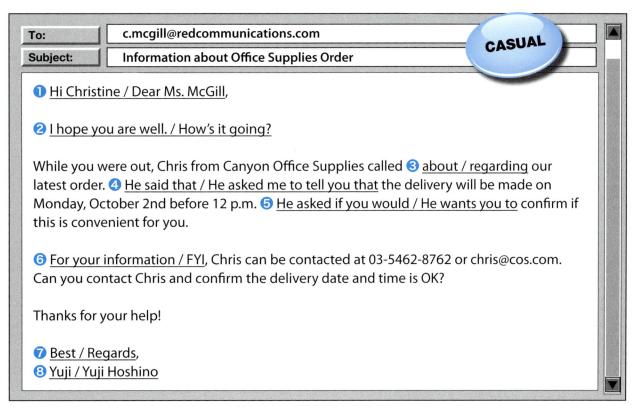

UNIT 15 | **Taking Messages**

11 | *Writing Task 3*

Complete the **SEMI-FORMAL** email from Yuji to a senior coworker.

To: a.hammond@redmagazine.com

Subject: Information about Next Week's Meeting

SEMI-FORMAL

Dear Allen,

I hope ❶_____ _____ _____.

❷_____ _____ were out, David from Classic Media called ❸_____ your meeting next week. ❹_____ _____ _____ to tell you that he is unable to meet you on Tuesday, so he would like to reschedule to Thursday at 10 a.m. ❺_____ _____ _____ you to confirm if this is convenient for you.

Please could you contact David to confirm the arrangements? ❻_____ _____ _____, he will be in his office all afternoon.

Thank you for your help.

Best regards,
Yuji

Business Writing Tip

Using Abbreviations

In both speaking and writing, you should be careful when using abbreviations, as they seem very casual. They are fine for friends or close coworkers, but they are not usually suitable for business communication.

For example, "FYI", "ASAP", and "BTW" seem very casual. "For your information", "As soon as possible" and "By the way" are more suitable for business communication.

You should also avoid using shortened words in emails. While they help you save time, they are much too casual for business communication.

For example, "tks", "pls" and "gonna" seem very casual. "Thanks", "please" and "going to" are more suitable for business communication.

90

Unit 1 Introducing Yourself

Networking

1. Conversation   32

Find two questions in the conversation with a similar meaning to: *What is your job?*

Miyuki:	I don't think we've met. My name is Miyuki Hara.
George:	It's nice to meet you, Miyuki. I'm George Winter.
Miyuki:	It's nice to meet you, too. So, what do you do?
George:	I'm a software engineer at JCN.
Miyuki:	Really? I've heard a lot of good things about your company.
George:	That's nice to hear. So where do you work?
Miyuki:	I work in the Marketing Department for PC Magazine.
George:	Oh yeah? I really like that magazine. Allow me to give you my card.
Miyuki:	Thanks. Here's my card.
George:	Thank you.
Miyuki:	Well, it was very nice to meet you.
George:	You too.

2. Useful Expressions

Add three expressions from the conversation to the chart.

How to Network	
Introduce yourself	• Nice to meet you. **My name is** Miyuki Hara. • I don't think we've met. **My name is** Miyuki Hara.
Explain your job	• **I'm a** software engineer **at** JCN. • **I work in** the Marketing Department **for** PC Magazine.
Make a positive comment	• (1) _____. • I really like your company's products.
Exchange business cards	• (2) _____. • Here's my card.
Say goodbye	• It was nice talking to you. • (3) _____.

3. Speaking

Role-play a networking event. Create some business cards. Then try to meet five people.

91

Unit 2 Introducing Companies

Making an Elevator Pitch

1. Conversation

Takumi is a sales representative. He is visiting an office to make an elevator pitch about his company. (An elevator pitch is a short speech that will attract people to your company.)
What kind of company does Takumi work for? What are the benefits of using his company?

Receptionist: Good morning. Can I help you?

Takumi: Good morning. My name is Takumi Miyata. I'm a sales representative for Bright Web. We are an internet service provider for the Tokyo area. Our best-selling package offers high-speed internet for a great price. We have also won awards for our customer service. Let me give you my card. I'd be very happy to send you more details about our packages and give you a quote.

Receptionist: Thank you. We'll take a look at your website.

2. Useful Expressions

Complete the chart with the missing words. Use the conversation to help you.

How to Make an Elevator Pitch	
Explain your company and your job	• **I work for** Star Electronics as a research assistant. • **I'm a** sales representative **(1)** _____ Tokyo Insurance.
Explain what your company does	• **We (2)** _____ a health insurance company. • **We produce** electronic components for cell phones.
Give some specific details	• **Our best-selling product is** a cell phone battery. • **Our** policies come with free health monitoring devices.
Explain your success	• **We supply** several leading electronics companies. • **We have (3)** _____ **awards for** our policies.
Suggest next steps	• You can read more about us on our website. • Please contact me if you would like more information.

3. Speaking

Choose a company and write an elevator pitch. Then give your pitch to your classmates.

Unit 3 Explaining Your Role

Introducing Your Team

1. Conversation

  34

Shizue is introducing a visitor to her team. How many people are on the team? What does the team do?

Shizue: Before we start the meeting, I'd like to introduce you to the rest of the Customer Service Team. There are five of us on the team. This is Toru Tanaka, the manager of the team. And this is Miyuki Ogawa, Nao Uchiwa, and Noriko Yamashita. We are responsible for assisting customers on the phone and replying to emails from customers.

Megan: It's very nice to meet you all.

Toru: It's nice to meet you, too. Please let us know if we can help you with anything.

Megan: Thank you. I'm looking forward to working with you.

2. Useful Expressions

Complete the expressions in the chart. Use the conversation to help you.

How to Introduce Your Team	
Start the introduction	• **Let me introduce** my coworkers. • **(1)** _____ the rest of my team.
Explain the structure of the team	• **There are** six **of us on the team**. • **We have** three sales staff and three marketing staff.
Explain the team's function	• **(2)** _____ processing invoices. • **We work with** customers in South America.
Introduce people	• **(3)** _____ my coworker John Smith, one of our buyers. • **Let me introduce you to** Junko Mori from the Sales Team.
Introduce people's roles	• **She is in charge of** the accounting system. • **He is** an administrative assistant.

3. Speaking

Role-play introducing a visitor to your coworkers. Imagine you work on one of these teams:

Team	Key Responsibilities
the HR Team	hiring staff, training staff
the Marketing Team	updating the company website, producing marketing materials

93

Supplementary Worksheet

Unit 4 Introducing Products

Making a Sales Pitch

1. Conversation   35

Yuriko is explaining one of her company's products to Michael. What benefits of the product does she mention?

Michael: Can you help me? I'm going camping in a couple of weeks, so I'm looking for a winter jacket.

Yuriko: Certainly. This is one of our most popular jackets. It has a fleece lining, so it's really warm. It's also very compact, so it's easy to put it in your backpack.

Michael: Sounds great. Is it expensive?

Yuriko: No, it's actually a lot cheaper than some brands – and it has received excellent reviews on our website. Would you like to try it on?

Michael: Yes, please. Can I try the black one?

Yuriko: Certainly. Here you go.

2. Useful Expressions

Complete the expressions in the chart. Use the conversation to help you.

How to Make a Sales Pitch	
Introduce the product	• This is (1) _____ of our new milkshakes. • This is the latest model in our range of laptops.
Explain the key features	• It's made from banana, strawberry, and kiwi fruit. • It (2) _____ a built-in webcam so you can use it for video conferences.
Explain the benefits	• It helps you to lose weight. • It's very light, (3) _____ it's really easy to carry.
Compare it to other products	• It's healthier than other milkshakes. • It's more powerful than most other laptops.
Explain what other people think	• It's the best-selling milkshake in Japan. • It has (4) _____ excellent reviews.

3. Speaking

Choose one of the products below and create a sales pitch. Then try to sell your product to your classmates.

- a cell phone
- some shoes
- a drink
- a car
- a book
- a bag

94

Supplementary Worksheet

Unit 5 Checking Information

Explaining Something

1. Conversation   36

Hisashi is explaining something to Julia. Check the things that he does to explain it.

☐ He compares it to something.   ☐ He explains how people use it.
☐ He shows her one.   ☐ He describes it.

Hisashi: Julia, do you have an *inkan* yet?
Julia: What's an *inkan*?
Hisashi: Um, it's like a stamp. We use it to sign our names on important documents. It's quite small, and it's usually made of plastic or wood.
Julia: You mean the thing that people use to stamp their name in red ink?
Hisashi: Yes, that's right.
Julia: Ah! No, I don't have one yet.
Hisashi: OK. Why don't I help you buy one after work today?
Julia: That would be really kind. Thank you.

2. Useful Expressions

Complete the expressions in the chart. Use the conversation to help you.

How to Explain Something	
Say what kind of thing it is	• It's a kind of tool. • It's a place that tourists visit.
Compare it to something	• It's (1) _____ a stamp. • It's similar to a palace.
Say how people use it	• We (2) _____ it to sign our names on important documents. • Rich people live in them.
Describe it	• It's (3) _____ of plastic or wood. • It's very beautiful.
Describe the size, shape or color	• It's quite small. • It's really large.

3. Speaking

Choose an item. Then describe it to your partner. Can they guess what it is?

• a shamoji   • an obi   • a furoshiki   • an omamori   • an uchiwa

95

Unit 6 Giving Your Opinion

Agreeing and Disagreeing

1. Conversation

  37

Simon wants to take some customers out for dinner next week. Where do they decide to go for dinner? Why do they decide to go there?

Simon: Where should we take our customers for dinner next week?

Mayu: Perhaps we should take them to the sushi restaurant on the top floor of that building in Shinjuku. It has wonderful views of the city. According to Erina, you can see Mount Fuji on clear days.

Naomi: That's a good idea, but I think the weather will be bad next week. I think we should go to the yakiniku restaurant around the corner, because the food is really good and people love to try cooking their own food.

Mayu: Oh yes, I completely agree with you. As you said, it's really fun for people to cook their own food. We always have a good time when we go there.

Simon: OK. I'll book a table. Thanks for your help.

2. Useful Expressions

Add three expressions from the conversation to the chart.

How to Agree and Disagree	
Agree	• (1) _____. • I think so too.
Explain why you agree	• … **because** it is really beautiful at this time of year. • (2) _____, it's really fun for people to cook their own food.
Disagree politely	• (3) _____, but … • I'm afraid I disagree.
Explain why you disagree	• **I think that** the weather will be too cold. • … **because** it's going to rain on Sunday.

3. Speaking

Discuss these topics with your partner. Do you agree or disagree?

- Should boys and girls study in different classes?
- Should university students wear a uniform?
- Should all students study English?
- Should students have a part-time job?

Unit 7 Making Requests

Supplementary Worksheet

Refusing Politely

1. Conversation

  38

Glenn is asking Yuko for some help. Why can't Yuko help Glenn? What does she suggest?

Glenn: Yuko, can you help me with something? Could you translate this document into English for me?

Yuko: I'd like to help, but I'm afraid I need to finish this report before the end of the day, so I don't have time to look at that now. Have you asked Hiroshi? He's really good at translating things.

Glenn: Unfortunately, he's in a meeting all afternoon.

Yuko: Oh. Well, if I were you, I would ask Laura in Marketing. Her Japanese is really good. She can probably do it for you.

Glenn: Good idea. I'll ask her.

2. Useful Expressions

Complete the expressions in the chart. Use the conversation to help you.

How to Refuse Politely	
Refusing politely	• I'm really sorry, but … • I'd (1) _____ to help, but I'm afraid …
Give a reason	• I (2) _____ to finish this report. • **I have to** take it with me tomorrow.
Offer alternative solutions	• (3) _____ **you** asked Hiroshi? • **Could you** wait until the day after tomorrow? • **If I were you, I** (4) _____ use your tablet instead. • **If you can** wait until Monday, I can help you.

3. Speaking

Ask your classmates to do these things. Politely refuse your classmates' requests.

- Do your homework
- Lend you ¥100,000
- Make your dinner every day
- Drive you to university every day
- Cut your hair
- Tidy your apartment

Student A: Could you do my homework for me, please?
Student B: I'm really sorry, but…

97

Unit 8 Asking Permission

Asking for a Big Favor

1. Conversation

  39

Nobuo is asking Jack for a favor. What does Nobuo want to do? Why?

Nobuo: Jack, can I ask you a big favor?

Jack: Sure. What is it?

Nobuo: Well, I'm giving a presentation to a really important client tomorrow, so I was wondering if I could work from home this afternoon to practice. It would be much easier to practice there. I'll stay late on Thursday to make up for it.

Jack: Sure. That's no problem. And good luck with your presentation.

Nobuo: Thank you!

2. Useful Expressions

Complete the chart with expressions from the conversation.

How to Ask for a Big Favor	
Explain that you need a favor	• Could I ask you something? • (1) _____?
Explain the background to the request	• I **need to** help my parents with something tomorrow morning. • (2) _____ presentation to a really important client tomorrow.
Make the request	• **So would it be possible for me to** come in an hour later than usual? • (3) _____ work from home.
Explain the reasons	• It's really important that I help them. • (4) _____ much easier to practice at home.
Offer some help in return	• I'll stay late to make up the time. • I'll also get started on the sales report.

3. Speaking

Try to find a classmate who will let you do these things.

- use their laptop all day tomorrow
- borrow their bicycle for a month
- borrow ¥50,000
- copy their homework
- use their phone to call the USA for one hour
- eat their lunch

Supplementary Worksheet

Unit 9 Making Invitations

Making Plans

1. Conversation   40

Rie and Paula are making plans for dinner. Where are they going? When and where will they meet?

Rie: Well, I think that covers everything we wanted to talk about today.
Paula: Yes, that was a really good meeting.
Rie: So, would you like to have dinner together later?
Paula: That'd be really nice.
Rie: I know a really good tofu restaurant we could go to.
Paula: That sounds great. What time shall we meet?
Rie: How about meeting at seven o'clock?
Paula: Yes, that'd be great. Where shall we meet?
Rie: Let's meet in the lobby at your hotel. The restaurant is close to the hotel.
Paula: OK. So I'll see you at seven o'clock in the hotel lobby.
Rie: Yes, see you then.

2. Useful Expressions

Complete the chart with questions from the conversation.

How to Make Plans	
Ask when to meet	• (1) _____ • What time do you want to meet?
Suggest when to meet	• **Let's meet on** Wednesday. • **How about meeting at** 12:30?
Ask where to meet	• (2) _____ • Where do you want to meet?
Suggest where to meet	• **Let's meet at** the station. • **Can you meet me outside** the office?
Confirm arrangements	• **OK. So I will see you at** 12:30 **at** the station. • **So, let's meet at** 6:00 **outside** the restaurant.

3. Speaking

Make plans to meet some classmates for these situations.

- having lunch together next Tuesday
- watching a sports game at the weekend
- going out for dinner on Friday night
- studying together on Sunday

99

Unit 10 Making Appointments

Arranging a Time for a Meeting

1. Conversation   41

Satoru is arranging a meeting with Helena. When and where do they agree to meet?

Satoru: Helena, do you have time today to talk about our training plans for next year?
Helena: Um, I'm pretty busy today. Can we arrange a meeting for next week?
Satoru: Sure. Are you available on Monday?
Helena: No, I'm in meetings all day. Are you free on the 15th?
Satoru: On Tuesday? Yes, I'm free. Are you available in the morning?
Helena: If possible, I would prefer to meet in the afternoon.
Satoru: OK. Are you open at two?
Helena: Yes. Would one hour be enough?
Satoru: It should be. Would you like to meet in your office?
Helena: Yes, that would be the easiest for me.
Satoru: OK. Great. I'll send an email to confirm the details.

2. Useful Expressions

Complete the chart with words from the conversation.

How to Arrange a Time for a Meeting	
Ask about days and dates	• Are you free **(1)** _____ Monday? • Are you available **(2)** _____ July 1st?
Ask about times	• Are you open **(3)** _____ 1:00? • Are you available **(4)** _____ the morning?
Ask about meeting length	• Are you available **(5)** _____ two hours? • **Would** one hour **be enough**?
Ask about the location	• **Would you be able to** come to our office? • **Would you like to** meet **(6)** _____ your office?
Confirm the details	• I'll send an invite. • I'll send an email to confirm the details.

3. Speaking

Work in a group. Arrange four times when you can all meet to study together this week:

- one morning session
- one afternoon session
- one evening session
- one session on the weekend

100

Unit 11   Canceling and Rescheduling

Giving Excuses

1. Conversation

  42

Mieko needs to schedule a meeting. Why does she want to reschedule the meeting?

☐ She hasn't finished her lunch.   ☐ She isn't feeling well.   ☐ She doesn't say.

Mieko: David, can I talk to you for a moment?
David: Sure. How can I help you?
Mieko: Well, I was wondering if we could rearrange the meeting we have scheduled at one this afternoon. I'm really sorry to ask, but I'm afraid something urgent has come up.
David: Oh OK. Well, I could meet you tomorrow at one instead?
Mieko: That would be perfect. Thank you. Sorry for the last-minute change of plans.

2. Useful Expressions

What kind of excuse does Mieko use?

How to Give Excuses	
Accept responsibility	• **I'm really sorry, but I** forgot that I have a conference on that day. • **I'm afraid I** am double-booked.
Give a vague excuse	• There is something else I have to do. • I'm afraid something urgent has come up.
Give a specific excuse	• **I have to** write a report by the end of the week. • **I need to** visit an important customer.
Explain that someone else has asked you to help	• **My manager asked me to** attend an important meeting. • **An important customer wants to** speak to me.

3. Speaking

Role-play these situations with your partner.

• You booked a meeting with a coworker, but now you need to rearrange it because your boss has asked you to go to a conference on that day.

• You booked a meeting with a customer, but now you need to rearrange the meeting because a VIP customer wants to meet you at the same time.

Unit 12 Describing Locations

Giving Directions

1. Conversation   43

Rupert is asking for directions. What is the correct way to the post office?

☐ left, straight on, right   ☐ straight on, left, right   ☐ right, straight on, left

Rupert: Yuuna, is there a post office near here?
Yuuna: Yes, there is. I'll give you directions.
Rupert: Thank you.
Yuuna: So, first you need to go out of the main entrance and turn left.
Rupert: Turn left, OK.
Yuuna: Next walk two blocks and take a right.
Rupert: Walk two blocks and take a right.
Yuuna: Yes, that's right. You'll see it on the left. It's next to a large hotel.
Rupert: OK. Thank you for your help.
Yuuna: You're welcome.

2. Useful Expressions

Complete the expressions in the chart. Use the conversation to help you.

How to Give Directions	
Explain the first step	• (1) _____, go out of the main door and turn left. • Go this way.
Explain the next steps	• (2) _____, walk two blocks. • After that, walk for about a hundred meters.
Explain when to turn	• Then, turn left at the traffic lights. • Turn left at the junction.
Explain any important details	• Cross over the road. • Go past the bank.
Describe the location	• You'll (3) _____ it on the left. • It's across from the hotel.

3. Speaking

Give directions to a place near your university, but don't say the name of the place. Can your partner guess the place?

102

Supplementary Worksheet

Unit 13   Looking after a Visitor

Making Small Talk

1. Conversation   44

Motoki is meeting a visitor in reception. Choose the topic that Motoki asks Mr. Stevens about.

☐ the weather   ☐ his journey   ☐ visiting Japan   ☐ Mr. Steven's country

Motoki: Are you Mr. Stevens?
Mr. Stevens: Yes, that's right.
Motoki: I'm Motoki Tanabe. Nice to meet you.
Mr. Stevens: Nice to meet you, too.
Motoki: Let me take you to the meeting room.
Mr. Stevens: Thank you.
Motoki: So, is this your first time in Japan?
Mr. Stevens: No, I've been here four or five times now.
Motoki: Really? Have you done much sightseeing?
Mr. Stevens: Actually, I went to Kyoto for a few days last time I was here. It was wonderful.
Motoki: Which places did you visit?
Mr. Stevens: We saw the castle and the Golden Pavilion. They were incredible.

2. Useful Expressions

Complete the chart with expressions from the conversation.

How to Make Small Talk	
Ask about the visitor's journey	• How was your flight? • Where are you staying?
Ask about the visitor's trip	• (1) _____? • (2) _____?
Ask about weather	• Is it still raining outside? • What's the weather like in your country?
Start a conversation about known information	• You're from New Zealand, aren't you? • You work with Judy Green, don't you?
Ask about interests	• What do you like to do at the weekend? • What sports do you like?

3. Speaking

Role-play escorting a visitor from reception to the meeting room. Can you make small talk while you walk?

Unit 14 Making a Phone Call

Answering the Phone

1. Conversation

  45

Kakeru is answering a phone call. What information does Kakeru ask for before he transfers the call?

Kakeru: Hello, Yokohama Finance. Kakeru Kuroki speaking. How can I help you?
Beth: Hello. Can I speak to Reiko Hasegawa, please?
Kakeru: May I ask who's calling, please?
Beth: My name is Beth Mitchell from MDD Insurance.
Kakeru: Thank you. And may I ask what your call is regarding?
Beth: I want to confirm the details of a meeting we're having next week.
Kakeru: OK. Just a moment, please. I'll put you through.
Beth: Thank you.

2. Useful Expressions

Complete the chart with words from the conversation.

How to Answer the Phone	
Greet the caller	• Hello, ABC Company. Kakeru Kuroki **(1)** _____. • ABC Company. This is John Smith.
Offer to help	• How can I help you? • How can I be of assistance?
Get information about the caller	• May I ask who's calling, please? • May I ask what your call is **(2)** _____?
Ask the caller to wait	• Hold the line, please. • **(3)** _____, please.
Transfer the caller	• I'll put you **(4)** _____. • I'll connect you.

3. Speaking

Role-play conversations for the situations. Use the conversation to help you.

	Situation 1	Situation 2
Receiver	Mariko Sato, Osaka Housing	Chisato Tokita, Fukuoka Shipping
Caller	Bryan West, SD Construction	Wendy Chen, Beijing Logistics
Calling for	Yuushi Kurikai	Renzo Kaneda
Reason for call	project update	questions about a proposal

104

Unit 15 Taking Messages

Supplementary Worksheet

Helping a Caller

1. Conversation

  46

Nozomi is answering a phone call. How does she help Philip?

☐ She takes a message   ☐ She lets him speak to Kazuo's assistant
☐ She gives him Kazuo's cell phone number

Nozomi: Good morning, LTC Systems. Nozomi Tanaka speaking.
Philip: Good morning. This is Philip Porter from DTT. Can I speak to Kazuo Ito, please?
Nozomi: I'm afraid he's not in the office today. Would you like to leave a message?
Philip: Actually, it's quite urgent.
Nozomi: Would you like his cell phone number?
Philip: That would be great.
Nozomi: OK. It's 020-4651-2894.
Philip: Thank you for your help.

2. Useful Expressions

Complete the chart with expressions from the conversation.

How to Help a Caller	
Ask if someone else can help	• Would you like to speak to her assistant? • Would you like to speak to someone in IT?
Suggest next steps	• Shall I ask him / her to call you back? • Could you call back after three o'clock?
Offer to take a message	• (1) _____? • Can I take a message?
Offer to give contact details	• (2) _____? • Would you like her email address?
Offer additional help	• Is there anything else I can help you with? • Can I help you with anything else?

3. Speaking

Role-play these phone conversations with your partner.

- The caller wants to speak to Elizabeth Dodds, but she will be in a meeting until 5 p.m.
- The caller wants to speak to John Adams, but he is away on a business trip until Thursday.

105

Useful Vocabulary List

Departments, Divisions and Teams

- Accounting
- Customer Support
- Finance
- HR (Human Resources)
- IP (Intellectual Property)
- IR (Investor Relations)
- IT (Information Technology)
- Legal
- Manufacturing
- Marketing
- QC (Quality Control)
- Procurement
- PR (Public Relations)
- R&D (Research and Development)
- Sales

Job Titles

- Administrative Assistant
- Area Manager
- Board Member
- CEO (Chief Executive Officer)
- COO (Chief Operating Officer)
- CFO (Chief Financial Officer)
- CTO (Chief Technology Officer)
- Director
- Head of Department
- Line Manager
- Partner
- PA (Personal Assistant)
- Secretary
- Senior Manager
- Vice-president

Workplace Actions

- to adapt
- to analyze
- to arrange
- to coordinate
- to conduct
- to delegate
- to develop
- to ensure
- to facilitate
- to inspect
- to implement
- to liaise
- to organize
- to oversee
- to troubleshoot

Types of Company

- architecture firm
- distributer
- electronics company
- engineering firm
- HR consultancy
- internet provider
- insurance company
- financial services company
- law firm
- logistics company
- manufacturer
- marketing agency
- recruitment agency
- real estate firm
- retailer
- software development company
- supplier
- trading company

Describing Products

- compatible
- convenient
- cutting-edge
- groundbreaking
- innovative
- intuitive
- popular
- recognizable
- reliable
- sophisticated
- stylish
- useful
- user-friendly
- well-known

Communication

- an app
- an attachment
- a broadband connection
- a cell phone
- a conference call
- a direct number
- an email address
- an extension number
- a landline
- a reply
- a speaker phone
- a text message
- a videoconference
- a voicemail message
- a webcam

Office Locations

- the basement
- a boardroom
- a cafeteria
- a conference room
- a convenience store
- a cubicle
- a hallway
- a kitchen
- a laboratory
- the lobby
- a mailroom
- an open-plan office
- reception
- the restrooms
- a smoking area
- a supply room
- a warehouse

Scheduling

- a day off
- to book a weekly meeting
- to bring forward
- to cancel at the last minute
- to cut short
- a deadline
- to extend
- to kickoff
- a national holiday
- on leave
- to pencil in a date
- to postpone a meeting
- to reschedule a meeting
- a three-day weekend

Meetings

- to be absent (from a meeting)
- an agenda
- an action point
- to attend a meeting
- a brainstorming
- chair (of a meeting)
- to chair a meeting
- to facilitate (a meeting)
- a handout
- to be late (for a meeting)
- the minutes (of a meeting)
- an objective
- to observe (a meeting)
- a presentation
- a progress update
- to sit in on (a meeting)

Connections

- an acquaintance
- a client
- a counterpart
- a connection
- a contact
- a coworker
- a customer
- a junior colleague
- a mentor
- a predecessor
- a senior colleague
- a subordinate
- a successor
- a superior

Job Interviews

- an applicant
- an application form
- to apply for a job
- a full-time job
- health insurance
- an interview
- a job description
- an offer
- paid holidays
- a part-time job
- pension
- a permanent position
- a resume (or CV)
- salary
- a second interview
- a task
- a temporary position

TEXT PRODUCTION STAFF

edited by	編集
Taiichi Sano	佐野 泰一

cover design by	表紙デザイン
in-Print	インプリント

text design by	本文デザイン
Ruben Frosali	ルーベン・フロサリ

In Partnership with	制作協力
GLOBAL BRDIGE	グローバルブリッジ

CD PRODUCTION STAFF

recorded by	吹き込み者
Caitlin Kelly (AmE)	ケイトリン・ケリー (アメリカ英語)
Daniel Duncan (AmE)	ダニエル・アキラ・ダンカン (アメリカ英語)
Jeffrey Rowe (CanE)	ジェフリー・ロウ (カナダ英語)
John Daub (AmE)	ジョン・ドーブ (アメリカ英語)
Kellie Elizabeth Holway (AmE)	ケリー・ホールウェイ (アメリカ英語)

Go Global
グローバル時代のビジネスコミュニケーション

2019年1月20日　初版発行
2023年2月25日　第6刷発行

著　　者　　Garry Pearson
　　　　　　Graham Skerritt
　　　　　　吉塚 弘

発 行 者　　佐野 英一郎

発 行 所　　株式会社 成 美 堂
　　　　　　〒101-0052　東京都千代田区神田小川町3-22
　　　　　　TEL 03-3291-2261　FAX 03-3293-5490
　　　　　　https://www.seibido.co.jp

印 刷・製 本　（株）萩原印刷

ISBN 978-4-7919-7184-8　　　　　　　　　　　　Printed in Japan

・落丁・乱丁本はお取り替えします。
・本書の無断複写は、著作権上の例外を除き著作権侵害となります。